# DEFYING CIRCUMSTANCE

## REAL STORIES FROM COLTON, CALIFORNIA

Copyright © 2012 Good Catch Publishing, Beaverton, OR.

All rights reserved. Written permission must be secured from the publisher to use or reproduce any part of this book, except for brief quotations in critical reviews or articles.

This book was written for the express purpose of conveying the love and mercy of Jesus Christ. The statements in this book are substantially true; however, names and minor details have been changed to protect people and situations from accusation or incrimination.

All Scripture quotations, unless otherwise noted, are taken from the New International Version Copyright 1973, 1984, 1987 by International Bible Society.

Published in Beaverton, Oregon, by Good Catch Publishing.
www.goodcatchpublishing.com
V1.1

*Printed in the United States of America*

# TABLE OF CONTENTS

| | | |
|---|---|---|
| | ACKNOWLEDGEMENTS | 9 |
| | INTRODUCTION | 13 |
| 1 | SHADOWS IN THE FAST LANE | 15 |
| 2 | A SONG IN THE MOURNING | 43 |
| 3 | PAYCHECK TO PAYCHECK | 71 |
| 4 | FULL CIRCLE | 95 |
| 5 | SLAYING THE THREE-HEADED MONSTER | 123 |
| 6 | LIFE ON THE EDGE | 143 |
| 7 | MASTER IN THE MESSAGE | 171 |
| | CONCLUSION | 197 |

# ACKNOWLEDGEMENTS

I would like to thank Jonathan Florez for his vision for this book and Josie Arrieta for her hard work in making it a reality. And to the people whose true stories appear in this book, thank you for your boldness and vulnerability.

*Defying Circumstance* would not have been published without the amazing efforts of our project manager and editor, Jeannette Scott. Her untiring resolve pushed this project forward and turned it into a stunning victory. Thank you for your great fortitude and diligence. Deep thanks to our incredible Editor in Chief, Michelle Cuthrell, and Executive Editor, Nicole Phinney Lowell, for all the amazing work they do. I would also like to thank our invaluable proofreader, Melody Davis, for the focus and energy she has put into perfecting our words.

Lastly, I want to extend our gratitude to the creative and very talented Ann Clayton, who designed the beautiful cover for *Defying Circumstance: Real Stories from Colton, California.*

Daren Lindley
President and CEO
Good Catch Publishing

The book you are about to read
is a compilation of authentic life stories.
The facts are true, and the events are real.
These storytellers have dealt with crisis, tragedy, abuse
and neglect and have shared their most private moments,
mess-ups and hang-ups in order for others to learn and
grow from them. In order to protect the identities of those
involved in their pasts, the names and details of some
storytellers have been withheld or changed.

# INTRODUCTION

What do you do when life is careening out of control? When addiction has overtaken you or abuse chained you with fear? Is depression escapable? Will relationships ever be healthy again? Are we destined to dissolve into an abyss of sorrow? Or will the sunlight of happiness ever return?

Your life really can change. It is possible to become a new person. The seven stories you are about to read prove positively that people right here in our town have stopped dying and started living. Whether they've been beaten by abuse, broken promises, shattered dreams or suffocating addictions, the resounding answer is, "Yes! You can become a new person." The potential to break free from gloom and into a bright future awaits.

Expect inspiration, hope and transformation! As you walk with each real person from our very own city through the pages of this book, you will not only find riveting accounts of their hardships; you will learn the secrets that brought about their breakthroughs. These people are no longer living in the shadows of yesterday; they are thriving with a sense of mission and purpose TODAY. May these stories inspire you to do the same!

# SHADOWS IN THE FAST LANE
## THE STORY OF LEON
### WRITTEN BY RICHARD DREBERT

The drugs they shot through my veins beat down the meth, and I quit jerking against the leather restraints. The distorted faces in the room looked human again as the emergency staff bellied up to my bed. Hospital white caressed me into a tranquil shroud of calm. Safe from my rampage, the doctor staunched the bleeding in my hands and arms while my family gathered in the waiting room. It was the last thing I remembered for three days.

ఞఞఞ

As a boy, Mama had placed her hand on my head and declared, "Leon, you'll be my little priest someday."

I smiled and colored pictures of Jesus sitting with little children on his lap, but when my brother came to live with us, he countered Mama's prayers to Mary about me.

"Be proud," he said, thumping his chest. "Act like a man, Leon!"

He put his arm around my bony shoulders, and pride burned in my belly as I slurped from his beer.

Mama, the 11$^{th}$ child among 12 sisters, learned her trade as a seamstress in Mexico City and worked in factories in San Bernardino to make a living. I had several aunts, uncles and dozens of cousins on both sides of the

# DEFYING CIRCUMSTANCE

border. My father had deserted my mother in Mexico City before I was born, but he showed up *sometimes*. I came into the world after he spent some time in San Bernardino.

My father put Mama through hell, and she never let me forget it. They had married when she was 16, and she had a baby the same year (who later died from an aneurism). A brother followed and then a sister. For a while, Mama lived on the streets of Mexico City, trying to survive, while my father indulged in womanizing, drugs and booze.

*Pride.*

In the barrio at San Bernardino, Mama prayed for protection around me, invoking her saints and angels. To save me from my father's distorted view of manhood, she dressed me up for Sunday Mass where I partook of my first Catholic communion. She bought me a Bible and taught me to recite prayers to the Blessed Virgin.

At our home on the main street of the barrio, Mama sanctified a perimeter at the edges of our tiny yard. "Leon," she said gravely, "you must not go beyond this line. It's not safe, understand?"

On Seventh Street, when I was a grade-schooler, we lived at the crossroads of racial violence. Late at night, bullets creased our walls; whenever gangs congregated on the street in front of our house, I fled to my room to hide. There was a stain on our porch where a man bled out from bullet wounds. When we left for Mass, we never knew if our TV or food or silverware might be stolen before we returned. Mama and I seldom mingled with outsiders, and she carefully weeded out my few neighborhood friends. Mama surrounded me with aunts, uncles and cousins as often as she could. My grown sister lived in another part of the city and came to see us often.

Mama sewed my school clothes and sent me off to elementary classes where teachers placed me in advanced courses. I loved to learn, and my sister encouraged me to study. She became my study buddy when she visited us in the barrio.

"You can be anything you want to be, Leon."

And I *wanted* to be a good boy.

༒༒༒

Marty, my grinning brother, rustled my black hair as I curled up against his strong shoulder. He was 15 years older than me and sprawled on the couch after working all day.

"We're moving away from the barrio!" Mama said excitedly.

I worshiped Marty at once. "You like that, Leon? We bought a house, and it's got a nice yard. You and I will be spending time together!"

When he lived in Mexico City, my brother emulated his mentor, my father. Now Mama watched the two of us, feeling helpless.

She silently prayed to the Virgin that her eldest son wouldn't lead her "little priest" into the empty life that she despised.

# DEFYING CIRCUMSTANCE

But she had some hope. A vital difference set Marty apart from his father: Her son would never desert her. He worked hard, and she could suffer Marty's lifestyle to get her youngest son out of the dangerous barrio.

My brother and weary mother bought a house in north San Bernardino, and Marty became my mentor. He taught me how to indulge in passions that men had a "right" to enjoy — but only after work and paying the bills. Sometimes I shot pool in the bars while he drank. Marty taught me to drive at 14 — he couldn't navigate home without me.

☙☙☙

Long before Marty moved in, every summer Mama sent me on a grand trip to visit relatives in Mexico City to strengthen my Hispanic roots. I especially loved flying with my big brother, who used to live there. On the way, he schooled me.

"Leon, don't forget! Drink only from the pitcher. We boil the water in Mexico, remember?"

"Okay, Marty."

I'd be *really* sorry if I drank from the tap.

In Mexico, life was different than living with my brother and mother in the States. At my Auntie's house, it took 30 minutes to heat the boiler before taking a shower. She lived in downtown Mexico City and bought our tortillas from a woman on the street who made them that morning.

## SHADOWS IN THE FAST LANE

But, on this summer trip, at 13, it wasn't the strange culture that turned my world upside down.

"Dad wants to see you, Leon," Marty said. The man I had learned to hate waited in his big diesel rig, idling at a truck depot outside of town. "He says he wants to get to know you."

"I don't want to know *him*, Marty! He treated Mama like s*** — and he deserted us!"

But Marty and my father didn't give up.

A few days before our flight back to the States, my cousins and Marty planned one last road trip, and I was excited. We piled into my aunt's car as Marty drove to the outskirts of town and parked at a massive gas station.

The row of gleaming semi-trucks roared against my emotions like salvos of artillery.

"Marty?!"

I stared after my brother who strolled to the café and soon came out laughing with a man who could have been *his* brother, but the graying hair gave him away.

My father extended his hand to me as I stood by my aunt's car with my cousins. "Leon! My boy." I hesitated and reached out … glaring at Marty.

Dad showed off his truck, a Kenworth with sleeper and padded leather seats. Trumpets blared briefly, and my cousins nodded at his cool cassette player. He tooted the air horn and then …

*Chapultepec Zoo. How generous.*

My father tried to strike up a relationship with me as I stood watching the monkeys, so I moved off to feed

# DEFYING CIRCUMSTANCE

peanuts to the elephants. He offered to buy me novelties, mementos — but all I wanted to do was forget this day. He used all his charisma to win me over, and after a sumptuous dinner, he flashed a few large bills as he paid the tab for my cousins, Marty and me. My cousins and brother thanked him profusely, and I sat in stony silence. I hoped that he got the message.

If not, he got it on the way home. He was telling truck stories as I sat beside him in the back seat.

"Dad, will you just *stop*?"

"What?"

The sneering amusement in his voice set off an explosion.

"Stop it! Can't you see I don't care? I hate you for what you did to Mama. I know what kind of man you are — she did everything for you, and you left her for whores! We don't need you!" I fought back tears and let all my 13-year-old angst run free, but lowered my voice to a venomous tone. "You're trying to buy me! Why? So you can feel better. I don't need nothin' from you …"

Later that night in my sleeping bag, I wept out all my confusion. How could he try to fill years of my emptiness by taking me to visit a monkey cage? But had I done the right thing, spurning my own father who wanted to reconcile?

Dad made one more feeble attempt to bridge the abyss of abandonment he had dredged.

He met us at the airport, and I ignored the gift he handed me. I sat with my back to him at the loading gate.

## SHADOWS IN THE FAST LANE

Marty hung back, and I watched him walk with my father to the main entrance.

It was the last time I saw my father.

On the plane, Marty apologized. "I'm sorry I put you through that, Leon. You never have to see him again." He stopped, and his face looked troubled. "Dad was real mad at you. Can you believe it? He thinks you owe him because he took a couple days off to see you … I told him to go to h***."

My brother was my champion, and I respected him, but Mother's power came from her long-term resolve and loyalty to me.

*Mom and I don't need anyone.*

At the airport, Mom's beautiful smile captured my emotions as I trotted to her arms. She held me a moment and stepped back. A Hispanic stranger at her elbow stood too *close*, and a little alarmed, I drew her away.

"Leon. I'd like to introduce you to Paul. He, ah, brought me to the airport."

Marty shook Paul's hand.

*This can't be happening.*

Paul owned land in Mexico, collected rent from apartments in Riverside and had a substantial job at a factory where Mother worked. On our way home, he stopped at his beautiful home in Riverside, a long way from my school, my sister and my house.

"How would you like to live in Riverside, Leon?" Mom asked.

What could I say? I had no choice.

# DEFYING CIRCUMSTANCE

൞൞൞

*No chores. No study buddy. No boundaries.*

My brother drank to loosen up on the weekends, but my stepfather drank himself to sleep. I started to slip from my mother's firm Catholic grip as soon as I moved into my own room with a stereo, a TV and a phone. I felt abandoned all over again. Mama's time and effort was taken up with another man — tequila in a wound that wouldn't heal.

I made it my goal to find friends, and Mom seemed pleased about it at first. My search took me from the school lunchroom to the streets. Riverside kids had a way of communicating that I wasn't used to. They *shared*. Someone rolled out what looked like a joint for me, and I smoked it like Marty's cigarettes — but this was different.

*My angst went away in a rush.*

I didn't hate my father anymore. I sat on a dirty rug with a circle of best friends, and they all loved me, and I loved them. In fact, I loved *everybody.* I didn't care what anyone thought, and I laughed at all the funny faces and strange voices in the room. It took a couple hours for the angel dust (PCP) to wear off before I could stumble home to my bedroom and crash. But I was hooked from the very first puff. And I had found my homies.

My new friends helped crank up my addiction. Pills, snorting, I couldn't get enough. I teetered at the edge of gang life, but no one could sell me on dying for territory or a street. I dodged in and out of drug houses, learning to deal, steal and wheel, always on the move. White, Asian, Chicano, Black — if you smoked or snorted or shot up, you were my friends — no matter what street you owned in Riverside.

"Sure, come over. My folks are gone to work. We can party!"

By the end of eighth grade, Paul and Mama fought over the best way to *reach* me, and I was nearly able to break them up. I felt numb to Mama's pleading and Paul's ranting over their missing cameras and valuables. Girls and meth (methamphetamine) had stolen my affections, and I was out of control.

Marty tried to help me when Paul kicked me out. I moved back with my brother and enrolled in high school, but only showed up for classes if a particular girl caught my eye.

Marty worked swing shift and drank all weekend, so I had plenty of unsupervised time to get high. My young neighborhood friends on the east side of San Bernardino were gangbangers now, and one of my friends had fought his way to the top of a local gang.

The hope of an unending supply of meth lured me in.

"You need someone to watch your back, Leon. We need to jump you in. You up for it?"

"Nah, Ken, I don't think so. Where can I score some stuff tonight?"

Ken looked disappointed, and that wasn't a good thing. "This is your neighborhood, man." But then he brightened and said, "Sure, I'll hook you up."

# DEFYING CIRCUMSTANCE

Back at a couple's home, his gangbangers hung out on the front lawn. Janey waddled around rubbing her belly unconsciously as her baby kicked. She handed her man, Jorge, a bottle of beer and sat down heavily on the stoop. Music blared from the living room, and a couple of black guys strolled outside.

I was about to go inside and snort a line, when screeching tires laid me out flat. Everyone else dived for dirt, too, and pulled their pieces, but it was too late. From a gray Chrysler a spray of bullets ricocheted off the porch railing. The car sped away, leaving us to take stock of casualties — there was only one: Janey slumped on the steps holding her belly, oozing blood.

I hurled bile into the shrubs as Jorge half-carried, half-dragged Janey across the lawn to a car. Threats and cursing added to the tang of spilled beer and marijuana fumes. Ken gathered his soldiers, and I faded into the warm darkness, shaking.

The two black boys were gone, too. The shooters — rival gangbangers — had seen them with us and sent Ken's gang a message not to mingle races.

Janey survived, but lost her baby.

I should have read the graffiti on the wall, but my addiction had me firmly by the throat. I was closest to my meth when I was closest to my gang homies, but one day, at one of Ken's crack houses, I was forced into a decision.

When I casually ambled into the backyard, a couple guys started pushing me, like school bullies. Faces seemed grim as I looked around for support, and I fought back

## SHADOWS IN THE FAST LANE

pretty hard, landing a few good punches, until two more homies hopped up to pound on my ribs. A couple more sets of fists closed me up like a jackknife, and I lay still, trying to cover my face as the blows kept falling.

Suddenly they stopped.

I tried to say something through bloody lips, but my chest throbbed too much to breathe. Ken stood a little ways off, smiling a little smile.

"You been jumped in!" Someone laughed, and my assailants reached down to help me up.

About that time, it felt nice to live with my big brother. After my beat down, I stayed home a lot, getting high after Marty went to work, so stoned that I couldn't think straight most of the time. Shadows freaked me out. Outside the house, inky, sinister figures darted close to the windows, hungrily peering inside at me. Their zoo of faces contorted if I stared too hard, and the beings spoke to me. I covered my ears, but couldn't shut them out.

"Hail, Mary, full of grace, blessed ..." In fear, I repeated the prayer I learned as a child. My religious words only drew laughter from beyond the windows.

Little did I realize that soon they would be *inside*.

Mom and Paul had taken their annual trip to Mexico City, and my addiction ripped my joints like barbed wire if I didn't do a line every few hours. I had been up for nearly a week when the d*** shadows came through the walls inside the house. I panicked when I saw their beastly faces, and I dialed the most religious people I could think of.

"Sarah, I'm really strung out! I'm seeing demons!"

# DEFYING CIRCUMSTANCE

My cousins, Sarah and Tonya, had spoken often to me about Jesus, whom I laughed off when I was sober. Now, the name of Jesus seemed comforting when they said it.

"I think I might be dying, and I'm seeing these ugly shadow people — they're saying bad things to me, Sarah. My heart is beating my ribs to pieces ..."

"Stay focused, Leon! Don't lose it ... here's Tonya, cousin."

"Lord Jesus, we pray right now that you protect our cousin, and help him."

Crazy Christians!

The only time good Catholics prayed fervently was when someone was dying! My body started cramping, and the shadows closed in around me. Suddenly headlights filled the room with brightness. My brother was home from work early, and I hung up the phone.

Marty watched me pace for a while and walked with me, helpless to deliver me from my misery. The sun came up, and he put me in a warm shower to settle down. When I opened the shower door, I crumpled to the tiles. Doctors declared to my family in no uncertain terms the reason I was ill: I had overdosed on methamphetamine.

I moved back to Riverside for my 10th-grade year of high school. Mom blamed herself for my addiction, and I wallowed in remorse for about two months before losing momentum in kicking the habit. One difference in my life: I fell for a girl in north San Bernardino, and now I lived in Riverside. Kathy wasn't just a one-night-stand, but someone I cared about, for the first time.

## SHADOWS IN THE FAST LANE

I had been dealing dope on campus at school to support my own meth habit, but meth was playing havoc with my body. Something seemed to be yanking on my organs and muscles after I snorted or sucked in the fumes, but my brain forced my body to accept the pain. Kathy wasn't into drugs, and I spent my weekends with her before taking a bus back to Riverside. One day I had to face a new reality.

"Mama, Kathy's pregnant."

My mother smiled into her folded hands as she sat at the kitchen table, shaking her head.

"I'm going to do right by her, Mama. I'll marry her!" And I meant it. I told Kathy, too. I suddenly felt connected to life in a way I had never experienced. I had a chance to do things right and show Mama that I wasn't like my womanizing father.

*My first child would be born in fewer than nine months.*

Why Kathy changed her mind, I'll never know.

"I don't want to have a baby, Leon."

I was stunned. Helpless. Crushed. I pleaded with her not to kill my baby, and her decision stripped my emotions to raw nerve as I realized that the god of my catechism stared down at me with rage for the *murder* I caused.

When Kathy told me she was seeing someone else months later, I put up a wall between my family and any other relationship that might steal into my heart. Never again would I allow my true love to touch a woman. I patronized my well-meaning cousins, Sarah and Tonya, when they tried to comfort me, but my father had been right all along: Women were for games, not real life. As for my addiction to meth, the cramps nearly killed me if I indulged, so I smoked pot and drank on weekends instead. It took time for my brain to straighten out, and I recouped my lost education by going to continuation school. I graduated with a 4.0.

☙☙☙

Norma distracted my mind while I dated another girl. I met Norma by chance at a friend's house, and she attended high school at Rubidoux, a small community outside of San Bernardino. Active in school and family oriented, something besides Norma's figure attracted me to her.

When she was 16, she had given her heart to Jesus, this spiritual being that my cousins talked so much about. Norma had the same qualities that I admired in my mother: steadiness, loyalty and faith.

But I lived my father's lifestyle, sneering away any guilt that touched my soul over crushing hearts for pleasure's sake. Women were part of a game that I played well, and I dated Norma while dating Rita, a girl I lived nearer to.

I got Rita pregnant and felt no remorse this time when I took her to the abortion clinic and put up the money to kill my baby. I could smoke pot or drink away any feelings, and I kept the whole thing secret as long as I could. Norma still loved me, and I felt less *dirty* somehow, when I was around her.

My job at a lube and oil shop, Grease Monkey, was going well, and my aptitude for specialized mechanic work brightened a path in my future. I talked about going to Arizona to UTI, a school where I could be certified in the auto mechanic field, and I might never have gone except for Rita's next pregnancy. This time she wanted to keep the baby, and her mother demanded that I do the right thing. I made plans to attend the auto school and come back to marry her after graduation.

I broke up with Norma before I left for Phoenix.

☙☙☙

"Come home, Leon. The baby's dead inside me."

Rita wept convulsively over the telephone, and I bought a ticket to fly home.

Physicians induced labor, and I knew Rita and I would never be the same. Wracked with guilt, I considered my life at 19 years old: I had fathered three children. Two were murdered in abortions; the one that I wanted so badly, God had taken from me.

*He's punishing me, and I deserve it.*

It wasn't long before I gravitated toward the one person besides Mama who was unshakeable and caring in my sorry existence: Norma. But as deeply as I felt for Norma, I couldn't ignore the evil voices that still governed my life at this time. The shadows had fastened upon my mind, and each one seemed to have a name: Lust, Unfaithfulness, Greed and Arrogance.

I smoked more pot and couldn't get enough booze to deaden my guilt for hurting all the women in my life and killing my children. Then Norma got pregnant. Instead of feeling regret, I seized upon her pregnancy as a sign that I had been given a second chance to make things right in my life. Maybe I could still make Mama proud, and perhaps God would slacken off his punishment for my past.

I made promises: "I can take care of you and our baby, Norma. You're my one and only. I'll be responsible. I'll treat you good! Marry me."

And to God: "Father in heaven, I can do this right, if you give me a chance. I'll show you …"

I was 20 and Norma 21 when my family and hers attended our small wedding in her mother's backyard. Mama had returned from a summer vacation with Paul, and I was shocked when I noticed her dress hanging loosely on her thin frame. I didn't mention it, except to Norma, who had all my affections as we planned the joyous birth of our son.

My brother and I weren't on speaking terms (we had a falling out over money issues), and I knew there was trouble when he called me at work.

"Mama has cancer, Leon."

"What? No! How bad?"

I heard him take a deep breath. "It's everywhere. She's only got a few months to live."

# SHADOWS IN THE FAST LANE

*I'm doing everything right, and God is still punishing me!*

While my mother fought for life every day, I gave up and renewed my contacts with meth suppliers. Mama lost weight, and so did I: By the time Norma and I attended Mama's memorial service, I had lost 50 pounds. Mama died two months before Lawrence, my son, was born.

God had deserted me when I needed him most, so I made a promise to myself: I would live like my brother taught me — take care of family, work hard to pay the bills, but on the weekends, cut loose. Do it all!

My pride invited evil shadows a little nearer to my soul. They rode with me to the strip clubs and loved to see me advance in my tech training — more money meant more drugs and booze. Lust clawed at my mind, and I yielded.

My marriage vows shattered, and Norma left me over an affair. I tried to forget her and little Lawrence, but no amount of pot or booze — or another woman — could replace the healing virtue I had experienced from being with them.

Why Norma took me back in my angry, arrogant condition, I can only credit to God's mercy. And God sent my cousins to tell me about the one who could take away my addictions and heal my mind — Jesus. They bought Norma and me Bibles with our names embossed on the front, and I decided to go to church with my wife on Easter Sunday. I sat in the back pew at Colton First Assembly of God, determined to be unaffected by the religious service. But it wasn't religion that took hold of me.

It dawned upon my heart that roaring down the same highways my father traveled amounted to suicide. After a very simple message in a drama called *The Power and the Glory*, I accepted an invitation from a pastor to walk to the front of the church and give my life to Jesus. I made new vows to stop meth forever, and I promised to be faithful.

But arrogance still boiled inside me. My life idled at another truck stop on the way to true freedom.

☙☙☙

I had been running auto repair shops for several years when I decided to open my own. My family of four children, Norma and I attended Colton First Assembly of God, and God had blessed our business from the start. My partner was a friend that I had known for years, and each day I prayed over the doors before opening. I included Jesus in my business plan, like he was a senior partner.

I figured that God needed to be involved in my business so that he would keep bringing in customers. My goal was to keep God interested in my enterprise by doing everything by the book: going to church, caring for my family, keeping away from booze and drugs and no more womanizing. The Son of God became my tool to achieve success; he certainly did some things better than I could, so I needed him.

But Jesus was more interested in possessing *me* than in

owning a string of top-gun auto repair shops. I had no clue that evil forces still lurked just outside my soul. Soon all my preconceived notions of what it was to be a Christian man would shatter to pieces. The Creator of the universe wasn't interested in sharing me with business, dope or demons.

The beginning of the end started when some real neighborly businessmen dropped by after closing time, with a little weed and speed to share.

"Name your poison, Leon."

My partner jumped right on it, but I refused the speed. I hesitated and felt "in control" as I took a hit of marijuana just to "network" with my associates.

The first thing on my agenda on the following morning was to find a meth dealer, and my old addiction hounded me as if I had never quit. Sickly guilt hung about me when I looked into my children's eyes. I stopped going to church out of shame, and Norma enlisted Colton First Assembly of God prayer warriors to bombard the gates of heaven on my behalf.

I graduated from snorting lines to smoking meth, to hide from my failure and ascend to greater heights of bliss. In the beginning, my partner and I had plenty of money to purchase a couple 8-balls a week, worth about $500. My habits revolved around the repair shop: Meth deliveries came to the front door like UPS, and after work I headed off to strip joints or to buy porn from local shops. Insatiable cravings never let me rest, and I begged my wife to forgive me, unless my meth and ego ignited in my head.

## DEFYING CIRCUMSTANCE

Then I hated Norma, belittled her and sometimes beat her.

As I lay in bed, day after day, trying to clean up, Norma had to sign employees' checks, until we were overdrawn at the bank. I stumbled into the repair bays, drained and pale, but customers aren't stupid. Who wanted a wiped-out drug addict to replace his brakes?

Norma stayed the course. She prayed for the father of her babies to cast off the arrogance he had inherited from *his* father. With Jesus, my wife stood in the gap, between hell and me.

I had short periods of sanity when I actually tried to find some comfort away from pornography and drugs. During one of these intervals, I sat in the back of our church and listened to a prayer meeting going on. Some of the people were standing in a circle to pray together, and I joined them.

After praying a short time, I felt exhausted and wanted to leave, but a little woman named Barbara stopped me. She touched my chest and said in a crystalline voice: "YOU ARE A VICTOR, NOT A VICTIM, LEON."

I had enough sense left to know it was God speaking through this Godly woman. I understood that I could never get sober myself, and I faced a choice that would decide my destiny. It was as easy as choosing which size wrench would loosen a stubborn bolt: I chose Jesus, even though my body screamed for meth.

The evil shadows had moved into my shop — I could see them when I was high, and I even talked to them sometimes. One day, while experiencing a drug-induced ecstasy and torment, I told them, "If you want to play, come inside me!"

Suddenly the demons all around me vanished. But I heard their voices clearly coming from inside my head. "Kill yourself, Leon. Leon! Your wife is cheating on you. Kill her! Leon, kill them all …"

On a Wednesday night I attended a service all strung out. I sat with Norma and my kids and suddenly walked to the front of the church. I asked to say something, and Pastor Jonathan handed me the mike.

I introduced myself, but most people knew Norma and me. "I am a meth addict. My life is falling apart. I'm asking for prayer for my family …"

Some men came forward and laid hands on me to pray. Immediately, I felt pain inside me. A tearing. I wanted to fight these men off, and suddenly two more men grabbed hold of my arms to hold me. I started to run, but someone had hold of my ankles. They were praying like they were at war with some force that bound me, and inside my stomach I felt a ripping away until I suddenly fell to the floor.

I coughed loudly, like I was going to puke, and the things/feelings/entities came OUT! I had come off a three-day meth binge, and I braced for two weeks of fever, shakes and vomiting — but when I stood up at the front of the church, I felt like I had never been high a day in my life. I had tasted God's unconditional love so powerfully that I wept — but I still held onto shreds of pride, just in case …

# DEFYING CIRCUMSTANCE

❧❧❧

My business was my downfall. I had gone two weeks without meth, and though my partner was high, I resisted, poring over accounts to find a miracle to keep the bank from foreclosing on my house and shop equipment. It got to be too much for me to bear, and my prayers seemed to go no higher than the ceiling. At home, Norma and I argued, and I knew she was at the end of her rope, too. I could tell.

"I'm high, Norma. I'm so sorry. I been out partying, and I'm dragging bottom." I held her hand, but I saw little compassion in her eyes.

"No more arrogance. I promise …"

Did she know that I was sincere? I got my answer when she stood up, grabbed the car keys from a hook and tossed them at me.

"Get out."

I went straight to my connection and bought a 16$^{th}$ of an ounce of speed, which I usually used up over a few days — but I swallowed the whole bagful.

It suddenly seemed like I breathed pure oxygen, and everything in the shop was bathed in lightning, vivid, in motion. I heard people talking to me, and I realized the shadows were back.

At church, Jesus had "swept the house clean," and now the demons wanted to move back in! Screaming into my head, they said, "*Do it* this time, Leon!"

I called Norma. "Keep the TV on. I'm going to kill

myself. It'll be a freeway chase, and the patrolmen will gun me down where I stop! You'll see! Suicide by cop!"

As soon as she hung up the phone, Norma called friends at church to pray for me. I walked outside my shop, a crowbar gripped in my hands, screaming at strange forms stalking around me. When I realized that I had locked myself out of the shop, I grabbed a brick and shattered the big display window in front. Laughing, I ran through the jagged shards, feeling nothing but rage.

"She's found someone else, Leon."

I flung the crowbar into the pickup and hopped in, bleeding all over the seats. Norma was expecting me. The kids were safely gone, and she was alone.

At first she looked worried at my wild-eyed appearance, but the compassion was back in her eyes. "Oh, Leon. Go get in the shower ..."

I misplaced the crowbar somewhere and did as I was told.

I seemed to be coming off my high, but the images were growing more grotesque as I finished up showering. I glanced into the mirror, and pallid-faced zombies stared from over my shoulder. They were standing in the bathroom with me. One more glance, and I grabbed the sink in both hands, ready to smash my head against the basin — but other calming voices spoke from the corner of the room: *Prayers.*

I stared hard at the tranquil images of people on their knees interceding for me, and I asked if Tonya and Sarah had come.

# DEFYING CIRCUMSTANCE

"Not yet, Leon, they're on their way."

My family drove me to the emergency room, as my mind wandered closer to insanity.

❧❧❧

The drugs they shot into my veins beat down the meth, and I quit jerking against the leather restraints.

Three days later I woke, slowly fighting toward reality through a tunnel of uncluttered thoughts.

My whole life played through my mind in seconds: high school, Mass, Mama's death, my precious Norma — people and events created within a divine order, like tools in a Snap-on box, organized and ready for an expert technician to use.

God had *plans*. I had been spared for a reason. He had humbled me, and my life had a purpose. No shadows darkened any corner of my eye; I heard no voice other than Norma, who stood beside me.

"How you feeling, Leon?"

"So *good*."

No arrogance remained in my soul. I can't explain how it happened, but Jesus replaced my pride with a powerful, wrenching love.

A day or so later, I was at home, watching the news, my eyes riveted to a drama played out hours before. After a high-speed chase on the freeway, a man leaped from his car and pointed an object at a highway patrolman. They gunned the man down in the street.

## SHADOWS IN THE FAST LANE

He had aimed a spoon in their direction. Suicide by cop.

It could have been me.

❧❧❧

That was six years ago, and today I don't take for granted a single moment that I spend with my beloved family. My life is a message to be shared, especially to a hopeless young generation.

"Leon, you can't just walk away! You invested your life in that business!" Some people cannot see the eternal picture like I do.

Perhaps they haven't been dogged by demons, or addicted to meth, or been rescued from deadly arrogance like me. I can't allow success, or enterprises, or dreams to separate me from Jesus ever again.

I turned my back on my worldly ambitions and never dared look back. My former partner disappeared with no forwarding address, and this next year, Norma and I should be within reach of paying back my creditors.

The bank foreclosed on my home, but we are victors, not victims! On the day we cleaned the house spic-and-span for new owners, God connected us with a wonderful landlord whom we respect. Norma and I had exactly enough funds to move our five children into a neighborhood full of Christian families. We have lived here for six years.

Jesus has blessed my abilities, and I work with fine people as a lead man in a busy diesel mechanics shop.

# DEFYING CIRCUMSTANCE

Each year I gain more certifications in the diesel engine technology field.

"Leon, you'll be my little priest someday."

Mama's dream for her son has come true: I lead my family in the worship of Jesus Christ in my home and minister at Colton First Assembly of God. For those who knew me at my worst, it has taken years to build a lasting trust, and I treasure their confidence in me.

*Loyalty.*

Pastor Jonathan and my Colton church family opened their hearts to Norma and me, from the very first day I warily sat on the back pew 15 years ago. These loving Christians have nurtured me to spiritual health and have given Norma and me opportunities to grow in our service to Jesus.

"Everybody got his Bible?"

Many evenings our family scrambles out the door and loads up the car with five kids, seven Bibles and boxes of teaching material — weary after a day's work and school, but happy and secure in our destiny. Over the last six years at church, Norma worked with a grade-school girls' group (Missionettes), while I taught a boys' fellowship group (Royal Rangers).

Norma and I felt that our ministries lay with older youth, and God has honored our dream. Now we teach 13 to 18 year olds from all walks of life. Each one knows my story, and they know that Norma and I really love them.

We're passionate about reaching young men and women who unwittingly sell themselves to the evil shadows that stalk the streets. Demons celebrate a child's first puff on a joint or first encounter with pornography and wait until the barbs go deep before they show themselves.

*Chaos.*

We see it in the eyes of youth. Their muscles are taut. Their tank tops and t-shirts scream out expletives. Piercings and tattoos affirm it: "I've been crushed inside, and there's no one that can rescue me!"

Kids strut in jumpsuits at a detention center or slouch in a corner of the church, arms folded hard across chests, and I know the hopelessness they feel.

"God loves you too much to leave you the same as you are," I tell them, and we share our stories. Jesus chips away the pride, and I watch in amazement as the chaos fades.

Victim or victor? With compassion and the wisdom of firsthand experience, we offer them the choice of fulfillment that lasts a lifetime and beyond.

And the shadows flee.

# A SONG IN THE MOURNING
## THE STORY OF DONNA RANGEL
### WRITTEN BY KAREN KOCZWARA

Something was very wrong. I knew it in my gut as I slipped into my daughter's bedroom, picked up the phone and dialed the number the detective had given me. "Yes, I'm calling about Joanna Lopez?" I tried to keep my voice steady, but my hands shook as I spoke.

"Who's this?" the man on the other end asked.

"I'm her mother. Look, tell me. Did she do something wrong? That girl! What did she do? Don't tell me she's in trouble. Is she in jail?"

"No, ma'am."

My heart rate quickened.

"Is my daughter alive?" I demanded, suddenly overcome with fear.

"Ma'am, this is the part of my job I hate the most. I'm afraid your daughter Joanna was … murdered."

*Murdered.* The word sank to the pit of my stomach where it exploded into a hundred horrible pieces and seared my heart. "Nooo! No, no, no!" She couldn't be. This couldn't be real. My daughter, my beautiful Joanna, murdered? Dead?

Still clenching the phone, I thrashed back and forth on the futon as the terrible, dreaded word rang in my head. *Murdered.* Maybe there was a mistake. I'd just talked to Joanna the day before. She was happy … she was alive!

# DEFYING CIRCUMSTANCE

"Noooo!" I screamed out, my anguished voice foreign to my own ears.

"Donna! What's wrong?" Ralph flew into the room and saw me flailing around on the bed, out of control. "Donna! Tell me! What's wrong?"

"Joanna's dead!" I screamed. "My daughter's dead!"

❧❧❧

There is a soundtrack to everyone's life. Sometimes the melody is sweet, sometimes sad, sometimes so joyful one cannot help but dance and laugh along to the tune. My life soundtrack was all of these things, and it is through the sad melody that I found that joyful song again.

I was born on December 8, 1960, in San Bernardino, California. My sister, Eileen, came along two years later, followed by my brother Jerry four years after her and, finally, my brother Brian nine years later. My father worked as a street striper, painting lines on the local roads. My mother tended to us children at home; we were all very close to her.

When I was 11 years old, my father announced he was going to build us a house in nearby Rialto. "It'll be big enough for all of us!" he said, beaming. "Gonna be real nice."

For the next few months, I watched in awe as a plot of ground became a slab of cement, a wooden frame and, finally, a beautiful house with several large rooms. My father built it all with his bare hands; we helped put the

# A SONG IN THE MOURNING

roof on the garage and added the finishing touches. The house would share a story of many happy times, but it would hide a terrible secret, too.

My mother suffered from severe depression after the death of her own mother, often popping pills to make the pain go away. I tried my best to do well in school and stay focused on my studies. On Sundays, we attended the local Catholic church, but the rules and rituals were foreign to me and didn't seem meaningful.

After graduation, I met a man and married. Our son, Eddie, was born in 1980, followed by a beautiful daughter, Joanna, in 1983. Over these years, I became more and more uncomfortable with how my husband behaved toward me when he drank. I finally decided to leave the marriage. Still, thankful for the two precious gifts, I set out to make a new life for my kids and myself.

In December 1985, I met Ralph. He was kind, thoughtful and respectful. We began dating and moved in together. In 1991, I got pregnant and gave birth to a sweet little girl, Keli Rose. I was thrilled to be a mother again and thankful to raise my children with a good role model.

When Keli was 3 years old, she suffered from a terrible bout of diarrhea that lasted for days. Panicked, I called my uncle Louie. "I don't know what to do. This has been going on for days now, and it won't stop," I told him frantically. "She's so lethargic and pale; I'm getting really worried."

"You know what? Your aunt and I are getting ready for a prayer meeting here tonight," he said. "Would you mind if we prayed for her?" The prayer meeting was supposed to happen the night before, but was postponed because of a pastoral emergency.

I had attended a few prayer meetings at my aunt and uncle's house and was fascinated with how easily they talked to God. They approached him like a friend in the room, not like the far-away figure I'd been introduced to in the Catholic church. I didn't pray much myself these days, but seeing how sick my daughter was, I figured asking God for a hand right now couldn't hurt. "Thank you, that would be so nice of you," I replied gratefully.

The next morning, Keli completely returned to her normal self. I called my uncle to report the good news. "I think your prayers worked," I said, laughing. "Thank you."

"Prayer does work," my uncle assured me. "Glad she's doing better."

In July 1997, my brother Jerry and his fiancé, Karen, requested that 6-year-old Keli be the flower girl in their wedding. Several days before the big day, Keli grew very ill. I took her to the doctor, who brushed it off as an infection. "Antibiotics should do the trick," he said, handing me a prescription.

But when her condition worsened and her fever spiked, I grew concerned and took her to the local hospital. "We're going to need to admit her," the nurse said, her brow furrowing as she took my daughter's temperature. "We'll run some tests and see what's going on."

I sank into a chair and watched the clock tick away on

the wall. Every minute felt like an hour as I waited for an update on my daughter. Around me, doctors buzzed by, announcements boomed through loudspeakers and machines whirred and beeped. As my little girl thrashed in the hospital bed, my concern escalated. I took a deep breath and decided to pray. "God, I don't know what to do," I whispered.

*Call Bob.* I sensed the words. Bob, or Preacher Bob as my kids called him, worked with me at the California Department of Transportation office. He always talked about God and prayed for people. I went home to change and shower, then called him. "Keli's real sick. She's in the hospital, and they're running tests. I'm worried," I confessed.

When I returned to the hospital, I found Bob hovering over Keli's bed, chatting away with her. "How'd you get her to talk? She's normally so shy!" I marveled as they laughed back and forth.

"Shy? I find that hard to believe," Bob teased. He prayed over Keli, and not long after, to my relief, her fever broke.

The doctor strode into the room and shook his head in disbelief. "That was one sick little girl a few hours ago," he mused. "Our tests showed she has E. coli poisoning. It looks like she's going to make a full recovery."

"Thank you," I whispered to Bob. "Your prayers worked." I was beginning to accept this prayer thing. Was it possible the man upstairs was really that attentive to my life?

## DEFYING CIRCUMSTANCE

Ralph and I continued living together while raising the children. I began work on the freeways with Caltrans. It was a demanding job, but I enjoyed my co-workers and the challenge each day brought. One August morning in 2000, as I set out cones for a construction project, a co-worker radioed me. "You need to get back here to the yard right away," he said.

"I'm busy right now. Just finishing with the cones," I called back.

"Just leave the cones, bring everyone with you and come back to the yard," he insisted.

I raced back to the van and sped back to headquarters, where I found my father and sister waiting at the entrance to the yard. Instantly, I knew something was wrong. "What is it? Is it Mom? Is it Ralph?" I asked breathlessly, hopping out of the van.

"Donna, it's Uncle Benny," my sister replied, her eyes filling with tears. "He passed away this morning of a heart attack."

My knees gave way, and I fell to the ground. "Uncle Benny?" I cried. I had just seen him a few days ago! How could he be dead?

"Donna, get back to work!" my supervisor hollered across the yard.

"She's just lost someone close to her," my sister retorted, helping me to my feet. "I'm so sorry, Donna. I know, it's crazy. He was his usual bubbly self on Friday. You just never know when it might be the last time you'll see someone."

## A SONG IN THE MOURNING

Tears spilled down my cheeks as I clung to my sister and father. I had loved my uncle Benny dearly. He had been like a second father to me, and his prayers had left a lasting impression. An ache slowly worked its way into my heart as I processed his death over the next few days. This was my first real taste of loss, and there was only more to come.

The following year, in January 2001, my mother's depression worsened, and the doctors prescribed strong antipsychotic medication. But she grew suicidal and tried to overdose on the pills, and the doctors quickly stepped in and took her off all the meds. Instantly, my mother suffered withdrawals. She began shaking uncontrollably and went into a coma. While in the coma, she had a cardiac arrest. The doctors brought her back to life, but her condition remained unstable.

"If she goes into cardiac arrest again, I think we need to let her go in peace," my brother Brian lamented as my father and siblings waited anxiously outside her hospital room.

I curled myself into the cold vinyl chair and sobbed quietly. My mother had fought a long, hard battle with her mental health all her life, yet she'd still found a way to stay strong. Was my brother right? Did we need to let her go in peace?

A short time later, my mother went into cardiac arrest again and passed away. We were all devastated by her death. She'd been close with all of her children, having a unique bond with each one. A flood of tears came as I recalled the many times I'd cuddled with her on the bed as a child. As an adult, we would still lie on the bed, flip through magazines and talk about family. Her presence alone had been such a comfort. Her laugh had been infectious and always put a smile on my face when I was sad. How would I live the rest of my life without her?

To ease my pain, I turned to prescription pills myself. Paxil and Xanax became my new best friends. I popped the pills from the minute I woke up to the time I went to bed. When I got home from work, I grabbed the kids something to eat and then locked myself in my room, where I spent the rest of the evening alone in a daze. The pills temporarily numbed the hurt in my heart and helped me get through the day. I missed my mother terribly, yet I couldn't see that the very thing that had ultimately taken her life was destroying mine as well.

The birth of my first grandson, Isaac, in 2003, was the bright spot in my year. My son, Eddie, and his wife allowed me to be in the delivery room as their beautiful little boy came into the world. "He's just perfect!" I gasped as I took the tiny infant in my arms. "I can't believe it! I'm a grandma now!"

That same year, Aunt Sally took me under her wing, bringing me to her church in San Bernardino. Over the next couple of years, she also babysat Keli when I worked. As I continued to attend the church, something stirred in my heart, and I wanted to know more about God.

I went home and told Ralph I could no longer live with him unless we were married. "If you are committed to me,

## A SONG IN THE MOURNING

meet me at the Justice of the Peace tomorrow," I told him. "We can get married there." I knew Ralph loved our children and me, but he was content just living together and not being married. The true test of his commitment would be revealed by my ultimatum.

To my relief, Ralph showed up, and we were married the next afternoon. While I was thrilled with my new husband, a dark cloud still hovered over me. I was fully addicted to prescription pills and unable to be the mother and grandmother I truly wanted to be.

The following year, in 2004, Eddie and his wife welcomed a baby girl, Lexie. I was ecstatic to be a grandmother again and especially excited about having pink frilly things around the house again. "We're going to have so much fun together," I cooed to Lexie as I cradled her in my arms. "Tea parties, dress up days, dolls, baking … Grandma's going to have a hard time not spoiling you!"

❧❧❧

In February 2006, Aunt Sally and most of my relatives visited another church, Colton First Assembly of God, where my cousin was being installed as the pastor. But I was working and couldn't attend. She took me the next Sunday, and we have been attending ever since.

I had spent years knowing *about* God, but I had never truly gotten to know him. My pastor-cousin spoke about him as someone who loved me and cared about even the smallest details in my life. Through God, he explained, we could experience true peace if we invited him into our heart. I'd tried to find that peace through other means — popping pills in hopes that the pain would disappear — but I now realized I only needed one thing: God.

"God, I invite you into my life. I know I've done wrong things in my life, but please forgive me. Give me a clean slate, and fill me with that peace I know only comes from you. Thank you for loving me," I prayed.

Suddenly, I wanted nothing more than to learn about God and spend time at my new church. To my amazement, I suddenly had no desire to take the pills. My three-year battle with addiction ended the minute I turned to God for help. Instead of weaning myself off the pills as I thought I'd have to, I simply tossed the bottles and never touched them again. "Thank you, God!" I prayed. "Only you could do this. I know you are all that I need. Please take this desire away, and help me be strong."

I continued to attend Colton First Assembly of God regularly during all this time. I fell in love not only with God, but with the people as well. I had never seen such genuine warmth, such generosity and such a love for others in all my life. I attended prayer meetings and asked God to show me where he wanted me to serve at church. I wanted to give back to the place that had invested so much in me.

"We need someone to help with the preschoolers in a girls' program here at the church," a lady told me after the prayer meeting one day. "Would you be willing to take it on?"

## A SONG IN THE MOURNING

I thought for a moment. I'd been asking God if there was some way I could be helpful to him; here was my chance! Yet the idea of a dozen or two squirrely little kids running around seemed exhausting. "You know what? I'll give it a try for a month," I told her with a smile.

To my pleasant surprise, I enjoyed the little girls immensely. I read them Bible stories, played games with them and got to know them by name. A year later, I was enjoying myself so much that I took on the role of the program coordinator. I also joined the church choir, which I greatly enjoyed. I now considered my church my second home and thanked God daily for bringing me here. I knew my daughters loved God, but I wasn't sure about my son. I prayed he would someday come to know the one who had changed my life.

In the spring of 2008, our church prepared for our large Easter production. One day, a few weeks before the play, I sat down with my son, Eddie, for a heart-to-heart talk. "Son, you know how much I love you. We are not promised tomorrow, and I don't like wondering where you will go if you die. I am not afraid to die because I have given my life completely to God and know I will go to heaven to be with him. I want you to go to heaven someday, too. Do you know where you'll go if something happens to you?"

Eddie grew quiet. "I've thought about it lots of times, Mom. I know what you believe. I'm just not sure it's for me, too."

I continued to pray for Eddie, giving him over to God.

## DEFYING CIRCUMSTANCE

"He's yours, not mine," I prayed. "I trust that in your timing he will give his heart to you."

The Friday night before Easter, someone tugged on my shoulder after the Easter production. When I whirled around, I saw my son standing there, a smile on his face and tears in his eyes. "I'm ready, Mom," he said. "I want to surrender my life to God."

I was thrilled at my son's decision and praised God for turning Eddie's heart to him and answering my prayers. Little did I know how timely his decision was or how profound the reminder that we may not have tomorrow.

~~~

Just a few weeks after that Easter production, my daughter-in-law called me in a panic. "It's Eddie! He's tried to hang himself!" she cried. I hung up, threw on some clothes and raced the five-minute drive to their home to find she hadn't called 911.

My heart raced and my fingers trembled as I dialed 911. "We need an ambulance right away," I burst out the minute the operator answered. "My son isn't breathing!" I took my granddaughter out of the room and called my husband.

The next few hours were a flurry of confusion and adrenaline as our pastor sped me to the hospital to be by my son's side. The paramedics arrived with my son on a stretcher and immediately admitted him to the emergency room. "What's going on?" I cried breathlessly, following the paramedic to the back room. "Is Eddie going to be okay?"

"We thought we lost him in the ambulance, but we got him back," a doctor explained. "His vitals are stable but serious. We'll let you know as soon as we learn more."

I slumped onto the cold concrete floor in the hallway as the minutes ticked by. Eddie's wife arrived, her face pale and distraught. "How is he?" she asked, collapsing beside me.

I shook my head. "Not good."

She took a deep breath. "It was horrible …" she whispered, tears filling her eyes. Her voice trailed off as she turned her head away.

I was speechless. I knew my son had been troubled by their tumultuous relationship, but I was sure he'd been doing better since he surrendered to God. I'd been so hopeful, so sure he could turn things around. And now he lay fighting for his life in the other room after trying to end it all. How could this be happening?

My pastor arrived at the hospital a short time later. "Oh, Donna, I heard about Eddie. I'm so sorry. Are you doing okay?"

"I'm okay," I said quietly, tears burning my eyes. "God is filling me with his peace."

My pastor prayed with me, asking God to heal Eddie if it was his will. "You know what? I'm at total peace. God is either going to give my son the will to come back or he's going to take him," I said, wiping my tears. "I just have to trust in him right now."

# DEFYING CIRCUMSTANCE

Eddie's 28th birthday came and went. But there was no birthday cake, party or balloons. Instead, he lay in ICU in a coma, breathing oxygen through a tube and still fighting for his life. I remained by his side, watching my beloved son's chest rise and fall beneath the hospital sheets, praying like I never had before.

"Eddie, I know this is hard," I said to him one evening. I took his hand; it was cold and limp in my own. "Son, I don't blame you if you want to go. I know you've had a hard life. If you go, I will help watch your kids the best I can. If you want to go home to be with God, take his hand and go home, son. I will be okay."

Hot tears spilled down my cheeks as I spoke to my son, not knowing if he'd heard or understood a word I'd said. An indescribable peace filled my heart as I turned him over to God. Since the moment I'd gotten that phone call, my gut had told me he was already gone. But a mother is never ready to let her child go, and though I trusted in God, I could not deny the terrible ache in my soul at the thought of never seeing my son open his eyes again.

The doctors ran several brain wave tests over the next few days and determined there was no brain activity left. "We could put him in a convalescent hospital on a respirator, but he will slowly deteriorate over time," the doctor us.

"You are not going to put him in a home!" I told my daughter-in-law adamantly. "If this is his time to go, it's his time." It pained me to think of my son, once so full of life, spending the rest of his days as a vegetable. I asked my pastor to come over, and he talked with my daughter-in-law. Together, we all prayed and decided the best thing we could do for Eddie was to let him go.

The night we lost my son was one of the darkest of my life. I cried heaving sobs until my insides hurt and I could not squeeze out another tear. I could not believe that my smiling, energetic boy was gone. Though the Lord sustained me with his loving arms, a gaping hole formed in my heart, and I wondered how I'd make it through the days to come.

On Sunday, just days after Eddie's death, I showed up at church to sing in the choir. Though I was reeling from his devastating death, there seemed no better place to be than at church with the people I loved. I took my place on the stage and sang my heart out to the Lord through my pain. "I love you, Lord, and I lift my voice …" I sang, lips quivering as I belted out the words. As I glanced out at my church family, my heart filled with thankfulness and joy. I had a long road ahead of me, but I would not walk it alone.

No mother wants to plan a funeral for her child. "Lord, how will I bury my son? I don't even have health insurance," I prayed in despair. "Please provide for all our needs."

"What are we going to do?" Ralph asked me as we pored over the dreaded paperwork. He had loved Eddie like a son and was devastated, too.

"God will provide, I'm sure of it," I told him confidently.

## DEFYING CIRCUMSTANCE

God did indeed provide above and beyond. Our church family took care of us in ways I could not begin to imagine. On the day of the funeral, my nieces and nephews arrived in Dodger jerseys at my request. Eddie, an avid baseball player, had loved the Dodgers; we buried him in a blue casket, clad in a Dodgers jersey and shorts. The funeral was simple and beautiful. We played Eddie's favorite song, "How Far is Heaven?" followed by the beloved hymn, "Amazing Grace." We also included the contemporary songs, "I Will Praise You In The Storm" and "I Can Only Imagine," which I found especially poignant as I endured the most treacherous storm of my life.

"You're at peace now, Eddie," I whispered through my tears as I said goodbye to him one last time. "I know you're in heaven now, and I'll see you again someday."

I waded through the next few months, going to work and church and attending to my family at home. Singing in choir was therapeutic for my soul as I poured out my sadness to God and turned it into praise by singing. When the nights grew long and the ache seemed too great, God comforted me with a supernatural presence. *One day at a time*, I told myself. *One day at a time*.

In September that year, I got another dreaded phone call. "My grandson's dead! He overdosed!" my husband cried. *Not again, Lord! Not again!*

My anxiety grew, and I began experiencing chest pains. One evening they were so great that instead of going to church, I turned my car around and drove myself straight to the urgent care clinic. One of my friends from church happened to be working there that night. "Oh, Donna, you don't look good! Let me get you a wheelchair!" She rushed me to the back, where the doctors quickly assessed me and administered nitroglycerine.

"We're not sure if you're having a heart attack or panic attack, but we don't want to take any chances," a doctor explained. "I think we'd better get you to the hospital."

"I'll drive her," my friend jumped in. She clocked out and helped me into her car. "It's going to be okay, Donna. God is going to take care of you," she assured me as we sped down the road.

An hour later, I sat in the emergency room at the hospital, doctors and nurses flitting around me as the machines whirred and beeped. They reminded me of the long, dark nights I'd spent hovering over Eddie in the hospital, and I began to cry. "Can you please turn that noise off?" I asked at last.

"There, is that better?" A nurse turned the noise off, and I breathed a sigh of relief. "We're going to give you something to relax you through the night," she explained. "We'll see how you are in the morning."

The next morning, the doctors asked me to perform a stress test on the treadmill, and I didn't pass it. After running more tests, they concluded I did have heart problems. "We need to operate right away," they informed me.

*Operate?* A lump formed in my throat at the thought of surgery. "I haven't had a bath ... I need to call my husband …" I mumbled, panic setting in. Just as quickly as I began to fear, God reminded me of the peace he'd sustained me with after Eddie's death. "Okay, Lord," I said, taking a deep breath. "You're either going to take me or keep me here. I trust in you."

The doctors wheeled me off to the operating room, where they put a stent in my heart. I was patched up and good as new. I was thankful to be alive, but there were even greater trials to come.

In January 2009, Keli announced she was pregnant. I was disappointed initially; she was just months from high school graduation, and I so badly wanted her to finish school. Keli had always been a good girl, not one to cause trouble at school or at home. "I'm not supportive of teenage pregnancy, but I will support my daughter," I told my pastor. "I know she needs me right now."

That same month, my circumstances at work grew difficult. One day when the pressure seemed too much, I called my pastor in tears. "I can't do this anymore. I can't go to work anymore, can't go to church anymore. I just can't!"

"You know what, Donna? Don't go to the girls' meeting tonight. We'll find someone else to cover you. Just come to the sanctuary, okay?"

"Okay," I said wearily. "I'll be there."

When I walked through the church doors, I crumpled into a chair in the back of the sanctuary. My friend Debra, who often prayed with me, walked up, her sympathetic eyes meeting my red, puffy ones.

# A SONG IN THE MOURNING

"You okay, Donna?" she asked softly.

I shook my head. "I don't think so. I'm just so tired and ready to give it all up."

"Donna, God has not brought you this far to let you go," she said sweetly.

Her words were soothing medicine to my weary soul. "Thank you," I whispered. The music started, and I closed my eyes, letting the words sink in as my beloved church friends sang out to God.

To my delight, Keli graduated high school that May with honors. My daughter Joanna, who had moved to Phoenix, came for the weekend to celebrate with us. We swam at my brother's house and went out to dinner to celebrate her graduation and Ralph's birthday. I was so happy to have my family together. The girls had taken Eddie's death especially hard, and I was thankful that in our loss, we could cherish the rare and happy moments. "I'm so glad you're all here," I said, pulling my girls in for a long hug. "It means the world to me."

As I dropped Joanna off at the bus station the next day, she turned to me with a smile. "I will be back in July to help Keli when she has the baby," she told me. "Love you, Mom."

"Love you, too," I replied, going in for one last hug. "Let me know when you want to come, and I'll send you money for a bus ticket."

A few days later, I called Joanna late at night to see how she was doing. She didn't answer her phone, and I figured I'd try her the next day. I got up in the morning and went to church. When I got home, a police officer was at my front door. "I'm looking for a Joanna Lopez," he said, flashing his badge.

"I'm her mother. She's been in Phoenix for five years," I replied. "She hasn't done anything wrong here in San Bernardino. What's going on?"

"The police in Phoenix are investigating something." He handed me a piece of paper. "Call this number in 10 minutes," he said.

The minute I shut the door, I picked up the phone and dialed the number. After the man on the other end answered, I introduced myself. "What did she do? That daughter of mine, is she in jail or what?" I asked, exasperated.

And then came the words that would rock my world to the core. "Your daughter was … murdered," the man said softly.

I screamed and yelled for the next few minutes, inconsolable as I rolled around on the futon in my daughter's room. At last, Ralph flew in the door, and I screamed out, "Joanna's dead! Joanna's dead!" Oh, how could this be happening? I was living the nightmare all over again!

At last, I realized I was still holding the phone. "I'm still here," the detective said.

"What happened?" I wailed. "What happened to my daughter?"

"We're still piecing things together, but it appears she was going out to a nightclub with some friends in a double

# A SONG IN THE MOURNING

cab pickup truck. They stopped at a gas station for some drinks, and a car pulled up next to them. They began joking with the kids in the other car, their joking turned into a heated fight and a guy in the other car pulled a gun and shot four of the eight girls. Your daughter was one of two killed."

Shocked, I listened as he reported my daughter's last few minutes of her life like a blurb on the evening news. My beautiful, beloved Joanna, whom I'd seen just days before, was now dead? *God, how could it be? First Eddie, and now Joanna?* It was too much to bear!

When I finally calmed down, I called my pastor. "You won't believe this, but Joanna passed away this morning," I told him through my tears.

"I'll be right there," he promised.

My pastor and his wife showed up at my house a few minutes later. Keli, who had been at a friend's, returned home, and we all sat in my living room, reeling from shock and processing the horrible news. My pastor prayed, asking God to comfort us through this seemingly unbearable time. "I'm sorry, Donna, but I've got to get back to the church. The service is about to start, and I'm afraid I can't cancel it."

"I understand," I replied. "Thank you so much for being here. You don't know how much it means."

A few minutes after he left, someone knocked at the door. When I opened it, I saw my entire church standing there on my steps! They hugged me, cried with me and offered words of assurance and condolences. "We're praying for you, sister," they said one by one. Several of them had brought food; they stocked my refrigerator and began cleaning my house. I was overwhelmed by their bountiful love and support. In that moment, I knew exactly why God had placed me at my church. He had known not just what I'd be able to bring to them, but what they'd be able to offer me during another one of the darkest days of my life.

"I'm just in awe," I whispered as I watched friends flutter about my house. Ralph and Keli were speechless, too, blown away by the genuine love of our second family. Once again, we were faced with an uncertain road of trial and pain, but our church would not let us go down the path alone.

The next few days were filled with more dreaded responsibilities as I planned yet another funeral for one of my children. I chose red and white balloons for Joanna's service; they had been her favorite colors. Two pressing thoughts gnawed at me as I released my beloved daughter. *Had she truly surrendered herself to God? And why couldn't I have been with her in her last days?* The grief was real and raw, but God sustained me once again, holding me up when I feared I could no longer stand.

Independence Day approached, and I found myself dreading the holiday. It had always been a time of celebration at our house, but I no longer felt much like celebrating. I began to fret about Keli, wondering if she was okay every time she left the house. I had already lost two children; surely God would not take my third child

# A SONG IN THE MOURNING

from me, would he? Fear pressed me until I could hardly breathe. One day, unable to take it anymore, I cried out to God.

"Please, Lord, take this fear from me. I put my daughter in your hands. She is yours, and if it's her time to go, it will be her time. But I will choose not to live in fear."

From that moment on, my crippling fear disappeared. When Keli went out, the tightness in my chest disappeared; I breathed a sigh of relief as I trusted God to watch over my baby even when I couldn't. Trusting God freed me from shouldering the weight of the world by myself.

On August 12, Keli gave birth to a beautiful little girl, Alayah. As I held her in my arms, I thanked God for the gift of life in the midst of so much loss. Though I'd once lamented my daughter getting pregnant so young, I now saw this child as a blessing from God, a reminder of his love, my rainbow after the storm.

When my doctor learned my daughter had passed away, he tried to prescribe me medication. I shook my head vehemently. "No, Doctor, I don't need those pills anymore," I said confidently. "I have Jesus, and he's my doctor now."

I poured myself into work, family and church, continuing with the girls' program and choir. But the gnawing question of Joanna's relationship with God before she died still haunted me.

One night, as I fell asleep, I heard her voice loud and clear. "Mom, you should see it here. It's so beautiful, and when you get here, you'll see just how beautiful it is. I love it here."

I opened my eyes, and they filled with tears. "Oh, thank you, God! Thank you!" I now had the comforting answer I needed; my daughter was in heaven with Jesus! I was confident I would see her again someday.

As I endured the grief process, I began to consider the man who had murdered my daughter. The detectives from Phoenix called me periodically with updates about the case. They had identified the man, but he was still loose, and they were collecting all the evidence and data they could. "We're doing our best on the case," they assured me. "We'll call you back if we find new information."

I asked God to help me forgive my daughter's killer. Though he had taken what was precious from me, I did not want to spend the rest of my life harboring anger toward him. I knew that Jesus had forgiven me for the many wrong things I'd done, and I needed to forgive this man, too. The moment I released the murderer to God, I was able to see him as a broken person who needed the healing that could only come from trusting in God. "I pray that he will one day come to know you," I prayed.

Though I had forgiven this man, I knew I still needed to seek justice for my daughter. *You are not ready yet*, I sensed God say when I asked him how much longer it would be until we found her killer.

"Okay, God. You let me know when I'm ready," I told him. "Show me what to do. Guide me to the right people and the right information. I will trust you."

## A SONG IN THE MOURNING

Joanna's case would be featured on the TV show *America's Most Wanted*, and I prayed that through this national exposure we might get a break in her case. While watching another show about U.S. Marshalls one evening, I got an idea. I called the U.S. Marshalls' office in Phoenix and talked with a man who promised to get the ball rolling on my daughter's case. "May God protect you out there," I told him as I hung up. *God, maybe this will be it,* I prayed expectantly.

One night while home alone, I flipped through the channels and heard the words, "*America's Most Wanted* will soon be doing a two-hour special as they team up with U.S. Marshalls." My ears perked up; I quickly called the Marshall I'd spoken with and left a message. *He will be caught,* I heard God say again. And once again, I trusted that in *his* timing, not mine, my daughter would receive justice.

In the following months, God placed many people in my path that had lost a child or loved one. I was able to share my story with them and comfort them as only another grieving mother could. "You can't do this alone," I reminded them. "That's why it's so important to keep going to church and surround yourself with people who can pray for you and be there for you when you need them most." I was so thankful I had found that at Colton First Assembly of God. I could not imagine my life without my friends to pray for me and hold me up on my weakest days.

As the conversations kept coming, I prayed about

starting a grief recovery group at church. In July 2011, I approached my pastor with the idea, and he heartily accepted it. "I think God is really going to use you, Donna," he told me.

"Thank you, Pastor. I pray he does," I replied. "This road is really hard, but we can't walk it alone. It would be so easy to go down a road of depression and isolation, but God isn't done with me. I believe he wants to use my story to help others find hope. He is the only one who has gotten me through these dark valleys, the only reason I've found peace in the midst of my pain." I paused, then gave a wistful sigh. "You know, some days are harder than others, for sure. I don't grieve for my kids anymore, but I sure do miss them."

My granddaughter, Alayah, continued to be the light of my life. Though my daughter Keli did not attend church with me, Alyayah loved dressing up and going with Grandma on Sundays. "We goin' to church?" the little girl asked one day, eyes wide with excitement.

I smiled and laughed. "We sure are, baby girl." Again, I thanked God for this bright and beautiful child who brought happiness into my home. Though I did not see my other grandchildren as often as I liked, I thanked God for them, too. In the midst of my loss, I still had much to be grateful for.

Alayah and I bundled up and headed off to church, where I took my place on stage in the choir. As the music began to play, I glanced around at my friends, and my heart warmed at their smiles. I thought of Eddie and

## A SONG IN THE MOURNING

Joanna, singing up in heaven as they waited for me. "I'll find you where Hallelujah and Glory Lane meet," I told them sometimes when my heart grew sad. I knew God would bring justice for my daughter, but more importantly, I knew I'd see my kids again.

I thought of the Bible verse, "Trust in the LORD with all your heart and lean not on your own understanding; in all your ways submit to him, and he will make your paths straight" (Proverbs 3:5-6). To this day, I take comfort in this verse, knowing that even though I may not understand the trials that happen in life, God will guide me through.

As I opened my mouth and poured my praises out to God that night, my heart swelled with peace. *This is for you, Lord. My song in the mourning, my hope in the storm. I sing for you.*

# PAYCHECK TO PAYCHECK
## THE STORY OF DOMINIC OLVERA
### WRITTEN BY DONNA SUNDBLAD

I pulled into the driveway at my usual time but sat in my truck for an extra minute. It was payday, and I was broke. My wife, Amy, expected to go grocery shopping and run errands. Now, I had to tell her we had no money.

I walked into the house exhausted. The low murmur of Amy's voice mingled with little Dom's giggles from the back bedroom. I walked down the hall toward them feeling like a condemned man. I found Amy stretched across the bed playing with our 15-month-old son, Dominic Junior. They were dressed and ready to go shopping. She looked up at me and smiled.

I took a deep breath, struggling with how to break the news. Her smile faded. "What is it?" Amy sat up.

I reached into my pocket, pulled out a $20 bill and threw it on the bed. "This is it until next payday."

Amy stared at the $20, glanced at our baby and picked up the money. Her dark questioning eyes searched mine with the unasked question. "The baby needs milk, the doctor, wipes…"

I pointed toward the $20 bill in her hand. "That $20 has to get it all and fill up the gas tank." I slumped onto the bed beside her.

We often struggled to scrape together enough money to buy wipes and diapers, but this was a new low. The reality of our financial situation hit us both hard as little Dom climbed from the bed and smiled.

"I guess there's nothing else to do but file for bankruptcy." Neither of us wanted this. Tears filled Amy's eyes with haunting disappointment. *I've failed.*

❧❧❧

I grew up as a shy, quiet middle kid in a big family of seven. Dad walked out on us when I was 14 years old. Mom was on welfare, struggling to do right by my siblings and me.

At 13, I attended a local youth group and looked forward to the outings they planned. I was still quiet, but a 14-year-old girl there caught my eye. Amy was a pretty girl — 5 feet 2 inches tall, with full lips, dark eyes and a beautiful smile. When I was 14, one of our youth outings brought us to a little league baseball game on a hot August day. I stood beside Amy trying to scrape together the courage to ask her out. Awkwardly, I said, "I have a question for you. Would you go out with me?"

She flashed a gorgeous smile; the breeze played with her dark hair, and she said, "Yes!" That first date on August 18 officially marked our going together. We spent a lot of time together and had a great connection. We loved sports, believed in the same things and attended the same youth group, but we went to different high schools. A year into our relationship, I told her I loved her, and I meant it. It was more than puppy love, and we became high school sweethearts who went to different schools. For the most part, I hung out with Amy and her family. We wrote each other letters, and we went out together on supervised dates, mostly with her parents. Often after church, I'd go to lunch with them and spend the rest of the day watching football at their house.

Shortly after I graduated, Amy and I were on our way to dinner. I fingered the engagement ring hidden in my pocket to make sure it was there. This was going to be a special night! As she drove us to the restaurant, our conversation soured, and instead of a romantic proposal, I blurted, "I wanted to bring you to dinner because I wanted to give you this." I pulled the ring from my pocket. "I want to ask you to marry me."

Amy looked at the ring, then at me. "Yes!"

It wasn't the romantic proposal I had planned, but it was the answer I had hoped for. We talked about how to let our families know and decided to take Amy's parents to dinner at Black Angus to make the announcement. As Amy and I sat across the table from them, she extended her hand, showing them her engagement ring. "We're going to be married."

They smiled, glanced at each other and back at us.

*Why don't they say something?* I fiddled with the napkin on my lap. "We plan to get married next year." I tried to ease their concerns about their 19-year-old daughter marrying a guy with a job that wasn't too great. "I promise I'll take care of her," I told them. "I'll do whatever I have to do to take care of her."

## DEFYING CIRCUMSTANCE

The year after I graduated we tied the knot. We moved into a small one-bedroom, one-bath apartment. Amy and I stood on the balcony overlooking the highway, and I wrapped by arm around her. "It's home." I felt on top of the world. I had a beautiful wife who I loved, and we had our own place just 10 minutes away from family. I held Amy close. "I love you more than words can say."

Amy and I didn't have the greatest jobs, but we worked hard. My job for a local supermarket chain paid $7 per hour, so I also worked a second job. All the crazy hours made it hard to spend time together, but we needed the money.

I sat at the table eating my lunch, between my first job and my night job. I was still dressed in my black pants, white shirt and uniform tie, when to my surprise Amy walked through the door of the apartment. She looked amazing in her black slacks and heels, but hurried by me and slipped into the bathroom. When she walked out, she came toward me with one arm slightly behind her. Her shoulder-length hair bounced with each step, and a smirk played across her lips as she stepped beside my chair.

I put my sandwich down. "What's going on?"

She presented a pregnancy test from behind her back to reveal a big "+" sign. I looked at her. "What does it mean?"

"We're pregnant!"

I pushed to my feet, and we hugged each other. Tears of joy stung my eyes. I was going to be a dad! I was nervous and shocked, but happy. We went to the mall to

# PAYCHECK TO PAYCHECK

buy gifts to break the good news to our parents in a special way: a crystal pacifier for Amy's parents, and one pink and one blue ceramic bootie for my mom. Everyone was happy for us.

As excited as we were, it didn't take long for the financial aspects of the responsibility of having a baby to sink in. Even though we both worked hard, we hadn't saved any money. "What are we going to do?" Amy asked.

After a year and a half in our own place, we decided to move in with my in-laws to save money. Amy's parents were a huge encouragement and support. They owned a three-bedroom, two-bath home with a split floor plan. With their bedroom at one end of the house and ours at the other, it gave us privacy. But it wasn't the same as having a place of our own.

Nine months later, Amy and I drove to the hospital when she went into labor. The doctor examined her and said, "She's only dilated a couple of centimeters." He sent us off to walk the halls for a couple of hours. The faint ring of phones at the nurses' desk, the bell of the elevators and the murmur of quiet conversations all blurred into background noise as I concentrated on Amy and the baby. After a couple of hours, her contractions grew closer together, and the doctor ordered her back to the birthing room.

I stood beside her bed and held her hand. "You're doing fine. Just keep breathing."

When Dominic Junior came into the world, I was in awe. *This is something that comes from both of us,* I thought. They cleaned him up, weighed him and laid him on Amy's chest wrapped in a receiving blanket and wearing a tiny blue knitted cap. The doctor finished up with Amy, and when the medical staff left the room, it was just the three of us. Amy and I watched little Dom open and close his eyes. "Can I hold him?" I asked.

Amy nodded, and I picked him up for the first time. He fit in the crook of my arm. *I have a beautiful, healthy baby boy.* "I'm going to take care of you," I promised.

At my in-laws' home, the room across the hall from ours became little Dom's nursery. Amy took a few months off from work to care for our new son. When the time came for her to return to her job, family members and friends stepped in to provide childcare. This saved us money, but the savings didn't show in our bank account. We spent more than we made, and our credit card balances reached new highs. I'd grown up in a house with seven kids on welfare, and for the first time in my life I had money — or so I thought. In reality, I only had credit. This credit was fast spiraling into debt, and we had nothing to show for it!

Amy and I had grown up going to a church and youth group that met in a hotel conference room. Back then I'd sit on those sturdy maroon chairs with my family and about 65 other people, but I never connected with what was taught. It's just what I did. After we were married, we continued to attend faithfully with our families every Sunday, but something was missing in my life, and this wasn't it. A few months after Dom was born, we decided

# PAYCHECK TO PAYCHECK

the conference room church wasn't the place for us. It was time to make a change.

Amy made a suggestion. "My cousin Johnny is business administrator at Colton First Assembly," she said. "He's always spoken highly of the church." We agreed it would be a good place to try.

With 8-month-old Dominic Junior in his car seat, we parked the car in the church parking lot. We heard the choir from outside before we even opened the church door. We walked into the huge auditorium with seating for 1,000. At the front, a stage-like platform was nestled within a two-story alcove inset with stained-glass windows on each side. We walked along the light-blue carpeting to a red cushioned pew and sat down. I leaned over to Amy and whispered, "It's so different." She nodded.

Everything about this church felt right. I loved the music. They had drums, guitar and piano playing an upbeat melody I didn't know. It filled the auditorium, and the pastor was interesting to listen to. "It's different in a good way," I whispered to Amy. The differences didn't end there. When it came time for the collection, they collected it in three baskets on a small table at the front. The people filed from the pews and went forward placing envelopes and money in the baskets. I stayed seated. I needed my money more than they did. After all, we had bills and lived from paycheck to paycheck. We never had money left over.

Four years into our marriage, while still living with our in-laws, our credit card debt swallowed us. We tried everything to get our bills under control and finally called a debt consolidation service for help. We paid them each month, and they paid our creditors, but it was too little too late. One payday, I walked in the door with $20 left in my pocket. Amy and little Dom were dressed and ready to go shopping. I didn't even know how to tell her we couldn't afford to go, so I threw the $20 bill on the bed and said, "That's it until next payday."

Amy stared at the $20, glanced at little Dom and picked up the money. Her dark questioning eyes searched mine.

"That $20 has to get it all and fill up the gas tank." I slumped onto the bed beside her. The reality of our financial situation hit us both hard as little Dom climbed from the bed and smiled.

"I guess there's nothing else to do but file for bankruptcy." Like it or not, that's what we did. I had let my family down.

Bankruptcy did relieve us of that financial burden. We had a fresh start, and with that I longed to get our own place and provide our own home for my family. When I received another promotion, I suggested the idea to Amy. "Now that we'll be making more, I think it's time to start seriously looking for a home." She wanted a house as much as I did, but with the inflated real estate market and our credit history, buying a house turned into a fleeting dream. Home prices soared, and so did my guilt about the bankruptcy. *I can't even provide a place to live for my family!* I despaired.

# PAYCHECK TO PAYCHECK

We didn't give up, but home choices were limited. Finally we found a 1960s, 1,400-square-foot home for $315,000. We walked up the two steps into the living room, through the small dining area and into the long galley-style kitchen with a breakfast nook. To the back left of the kitchen and two steps down was an add-on den with a bay window.

"I like the coziness of this room," I said, brushing my fingers along the white window trim, then resting my hand above the wainscoting. The view from the bay window showed off the backyard, which stretched 20 yards through a canopy of trees to a fence. The grass and trees offered beauty and privacy. The room was longer than it was wide, and I imagined our family spending a lot of time in it. That room clinched it for us. We bought the house and put everything we had into the older home. *This is our house,* I thought, but in reality, it was the bank's house, and it cost us $2,300 a month.

It was nice to have our own place again after all those years, but we had to decide what to do about childcare for Dominic. Amy and I called different daycare centers in the area. We discussed each option: how many days, what times Amy or I would have to get off work. "It won't be easy, but we can possibly work things around." Amy nibbled the corner of her lip. "But it's going to cost $500 to $600 a month."

I shook my head. "We just don't have it." Still, we had to struggle to make things work.

We painted the den Dodger blue and decorated with

the little bit of team memorabilia we owned. With our new home, we settled into a new routine. Most evenings we'd come home from a hard day's work, have dinner and watch a movie in the den.

I enjoyed the freedom of owning a home. I had my own backyard and garage. As the man of the house, I'd never lived in a situation where I could drink a beer whenever I wanted. It wasn't part of my life growing up, or in high school, but when I was 24, I started drinking with my friends at ballgames or having a beer with my brothers. I decided to keep the refrigerator stocked with beer in case I wanted one. I only drank one or two beers after work, but Amy didn't like it. She didn't even want beer in the house.

"I don't want you drinking." Her brown eyes met mine. "When you drink, you're not emotionally there for your family." She hated to even see a beer in my hand.

"I'm not doing anything wrong! I'm home! I'm not getting drunk!" I took a swig of beer, walked away and went to the backyard. I was a man … a grownup. I could do what I wanted when I wanted. I started going out with my friends more, where I could drink and she wasn't there to watch me. For me, it wasn't about getting drunk. It was about doing what I wanted to do.

Our financial problems and disagreements pulled Amy and me apart. We lived in the same house, but that was about it. Each night we climbed into bed without saying a word to each other. In the morning we left for work without talking. To avoid the hassle about my drinking, I started going out with my buddies on a regular basis. Short-term satisfaction was all that mattered, because in the long-term, the satisfaction had evaporated.

Bills piled up and overwhelmed me. We struggled to make the exorbitant house payment on top of our credit card debt and car payments. I called the mortgage company, but it didn't help. We fell behind, and the amount we owed multiplied. Our finances consumed every part of us. At lunchtime, I'd walk out to the parking lot to my green Ford Explorer to make phone calls on my cell phone. I loosened my tie, unbuttoned the top button of my white dress shirt and pulled out the paperwork I needed to try to negotiate with our creditors. I was transferred from department to department as I tried to get payments added to the back of my loans. The creditors promised to help each time, but eventually they couldn't work with me anymore.

I sat at our sturdy wood dining room table with the bills and overdue notices spread across the surface, trying to figure out how I could juggle payments. I held up a bill to Amy. "If we pay this one late," I grabbed another, "we can pay this one now."

At night Amy and I lay in bed in total silence. She cried, and I felt depressed. I made it a habit to fall asleep early before Amy came to bed each night to avoid talking about it. Some nights I'd go to sleep before Dominic had his bath and left his bedtime routine to Amy. But in the morning, I never left the house without kissing our son goodbye.

# DEFYING CIRCUMSTANCE

Then the thing I feared most happened. I opened the envelope and held the foreclosure notice in my shaking hand. I read it and re-read it, and even though I had known it was coming, the official notice took the breath right out of me. I handed the notice to Amy. Her eyes filled with tears, and she ran to our room crying. It was our Dooms Day; we had lost the house after only seven months.

We found a rental home just 10 miles away for $1,600 a month. It was a newer house with three bedrooms and two baths — more room than we had in the home we lost. I thought I'd be happy once we were out from under the financial burden of our mortgage, but the guilt of losing the house killed me inside. We'd been married six years, gone bankrupt and lost our home. Losing the house embarrassed Amy. As the man of the house, I wanted to provide the best. Instead I'd put her through a nightmare, losing everything.

Shortly after the move, I walked in the door from work and found a card from Amy on our bed. I tore the envelope open and read the message written in Amy's handwriting. *It's been a long time coming, but here we go again. I'm pregnant. All my love, Amy.* Under her message, she taped the plus sign from the pregnancy kit box. With the foreclosure behind us, we hoped to do better. She was more excited than I was. In her way of thinking, this baby would show everyone we were happy and more in love than ever. No one even realized we had issues because we'd kept them to ourselves.

# PAYCHECK TO PAYCHECK

Even with a baby on the way, I'd look at Amy and think, *I'm a failure.* Tension blanketed our household as I considered the added responsibility of a second child. I couldn't deal with it. I needed to get away from it. One night after work, I grabbed my coat and headed out the door to be with my friends, leaving Amy holding little Dom in the living room.

Going out with my buddies became a habit. I hung out with them more, and I drank more. Even when I stayed home, Amy and I were like strangers in the same house. When it was time to tuck Dominic in at night, Amy went in first to say goodnight, and when she finished, I went in to kiss him goodnight.

As much as I struggled, I hoped the baby's arrival might help things improve between us. Brooklynn Nikole arrived, and Dominic had a baby sister. I had two beautiful kids. Holding my new baby daughter stirred such love, but didn't cure my inner turmoil. As I looked around the house, I wondered, *Do I even want to be here? Do I want to continue in this relationship with my wife?*

My discontent put me on edge. When Brooklynn was about 6 months old, I arrived home from work and went in the bedroom to change for baseball practice. Amy came into the room, sat on the recliner next to the bed and poured her heart out. "I love you. You are everything I ever wanted." She stood and followed me around the room. "Please tell me what I can do to help — to help us." I side-stepped her and went into the bathroom. She trailed behind me. "Why are you so upset with me all the time?"

# DEFYING CIRCUMSTANCE

I spun around to face her. "I don't love you anymore!" I turned off the bathroom light and walked out. Amy didn't follow, but stayed behind in the dark bathroom. Her quiet sobs clawed at my heart, but I shook it off and walked out.

That night, as I drove my truck to hang out with friends, the green light from the stereo system cast an eerie glow across my reflection in the rearview mirror. I turned the mirror to face myself and stared at the man on the other side. Raw emotions overwhelmed me. A guttural yell tore from my throat, releasing a flood of tears from my eyes. I looked into the mirror and shouted, "What are you doing?!" Tears stung my eyes as I bawled. "Why are you doing this?!" My voice trailed off into sobs. I fought to pull myself together.

My words to Amy that night had cut deep. After that we drifted further apart. Our underlying problems festered. Keeping beer in the house and going out whenever I wanted hurt her, too. But this wasn't the man I wanted to be. I'd look at my beautiful wife and long for what we once had. I had failed.

Our disappointments raised a barrier between us and escalated into disagreements behind closed doors, away from our son and daughter. Our disputes never blew up into full-fledged arguments, but they festered as private conflicts that ate at what was left of our relationship. Something had to change.

I thought about how much happier we were when we had less responsibility. One night as we lay side by side in our queen-sized bed, I said, "Maybe if we get rid of all these responsibilities, the tension will ease up."

Amy turned her head to look at me. "Would you be willing to move back in with my parents, if they'll have us?"

I rolled onto my side to face her. "I'd be willing to do that; it might help."

Amy talked with her father. "If we could move back in, we can save some money and get on our feet." Still, we kept our secret that our marriage was about to implode. We never even talked back to one another in front of other people. I felt that our marriage and relationship was our business. Even though no one questioned our relationship, I didn't want to give anyone reason for concern.

To our relief, Amy's parents welcomed us into their home again. We put all our belongings, except for our mattresses, dressers and TV, into storage.

Living with them brought about a change in my lifestyle. I didn't disrespect my in-laws by keeping beer in the fridge, and I cut back on how often I went out with my buddies.

Moving in with my in-laws eliminated most of our financial responsibilities, but I was still not happy. Even with the added support and encouragement, Amy and I didn't hold much hope for saving our marriage. Endless doubts bombarded my thinking, and depression set in. Thoughts of suicide crossed my mind. *I can just take my truck and crash into something.* If I ended my life, I'd put a stop to all my wife's trouble and pain.

## DEFYING CIRCUMSTANCE

The usual silence hung between us as we lay in bed one night. Amy pulled the covers up tighter. "I went to see a divorce lawyer," she said flatly. Her face matched the seriousness of her tone. She wanted to hurt me as much as I hurt her. I couldn't blame her, but she had never threatened divorce before. My mind raced. *She's always been there for me — always supported me.* A million emotions clashed inside me as her statement sunk in. *I can't blame her after everything I've done.*

I didn't know what to say. She had every right to want a divorce. I finally said, "Okay, if this is what you decide to do, then I don't blame you."

My answer surprised her a little. We started to talk. The more we talked it became clear we weren't quite ready to call it quits, but we didn't hold much hope, either. Amy let out a long sigh. "I'm not sure our marriage is salvageable."

We turned off the light, and I lay awake staring into the darkness, realizing she had finally given up.

*Even if we separate, I can still see my son and daughter. I can still be a good dad.* That thought weighed heavy on me, though. My dad walked out on seven kids. I didn't want that for my children. Just the thought of waking up in the morning and not being able to kiss them stopped me from leaving, but *something* had to change. Conflict tore at me, and the inner battle left me depressed. I couldn't blame Amy for wanting to walk away. I hated who I had become. I'd stare at the clean-cut guy in the mirror and think, *I hate who you are; I hate who you've*

## PAYCHECK TO PAYCHECK

*become. You're about to lose the best thing that's ever happened to you.*

I was losing it all: my home, my marriage, my self-respect. My drinking and neglect had pushed Amy past her limit. As these realities hit me like a freight train, I determined to fix things. I would fight with all that was within me to regain Amy's trust and be the man she deserved. I only hoped it wasn't too late to win her heart back.

Night after night, we sat on the queen-sized mattress in our bedroom and tried to talk things out. One night, I stared at the stains on the off-white carpet; tell-tale dribble marks from the kids' drinks. "Amy, we have two beautiful kids. We haven't burned any bridges with our families," I began.

I looked into her deep brown eyes. "I want to give this a shot, just take it day by day."

"Well, I'm willing to let you try to prove it," she said, shrugging. I had given her every reason to quit on me. This was more than I deserved, and I was thankful for it.

Everyday life didn't change much. We continued to go to work, come home and attend church on Sundays and Wednesdays. Then one Sunday, something different happened to me. The pastor's sermon seemed to be written just for me. He talked about "giving it all to God and letting him take control." Then he said, "If you're not going to do this for yourself, at least do it for your kids." That statement hit me like a two-by-four in my heart. When he finished talking, he stepped down from the platform and stood at the front of the auditorium. "If you are ready to let go and give yourself over to God, come forward," he beckoned.

I felt so empty. I stood at a fork in the road. My dad had the option to stay and work things out or leave, and he walked out and didn't come back. *I can't leave my family.* Something compelled me to walk up to the front. I took Amy's hand. It felt like God himself drew us out of the pew. I had to go up there. Hand-in-hand, we walked along the light-blue carpet. The orchestra played softly, and sunlight filtered through the stained-glass windows at the front of the church. I literally felt like God was standing there as I prayed, "Lord, forgive me." My hair stood up. I felt God ripping my past and all my mistakes away, from the top of my head to the bottom of my feet. My legs wobbled, as I swayed beside Amy. I had my head down and held her hand and started crying. I let go of the weight of my failure and hurt, and God stripped it away. I felt clean.

Plenty of other people came to the front, and the pastor prayed for each of us. I didn't care who else was watching. For me, it was a private moment with God. I prayed God would take control of my life. I certainly hadn't done a good job on my own.

With God's help, I followed through with my promise to Amy. It took about a year and a half of changing my ways to win Amy's heart back.

"Dominic," Amy said, "I didn't tell you earlier, but while I was getting ready for church, as I talked to God, I knew I had to let go of the heartbreak and bitterness. It was too much to bear, and I let it go into God's hands. My anger, pain and hurt are gone, but it's still going to be a day-by-day process to heal our marriage." I looked at my beautiful wife. She wore her hair down and curled, my favorite style. She was the most beautiful vision I'd ever seen.

"I agree," I said.

We both desired to do things differently, but we didn't know what to expect. Amy still struggled with the hurt, but turned to God each day to help her forgive me. We talked through things instead of harboring our hurts and depression. As we let God lead us through the healing process, we learned we were expecting baby number three! Our relationship healed gradually, and little by little we reconciled the years of hurt. God healed our marriage.

Instead of just showing up at church, we started to help out. I volunteered to be an usher. I went to church on Sunday morning, Sunday night and Wednesdays because I *wanted* to, not because it was a family tradition. I gradually accepted more responsibilities at church and even presented announcements in front of the congregation each week. This was a big accomplishment for me because I am naturally shy!

We still made good money and were only paying minimal rent to my in-laws. Yet, the balance in our savings was next to nothing. During his sermon one Sunday, the pastor explained that in the Bible, God promises to take care of us financially if we trust him with our money. It says that we can demonstrate our trust by giving back a tenth of what he provides to us to the church. Our pastor challenged us, asking, "Would you rather your 100 percent of income be cursed, or would you rather give God 10 percent and have him bless your 90 percent?" Amy and I wanted to walk in God's blessing and teach our children to do the same. We realized that day that we had released our marriage troubles to God, but still needed to release our financial nightmare to him, too.

"God wants to be first in our finances," I said to Amy after church. She agreed, but we both knew it would be a painful adjustment. The next week we wrote a check for a tenth of our weekly income. That Sunday, when people stepped from the pews to bring an offering to the front, I stood and walked with them. I placed the envelope in the basket, praying that I was doing the right thing. We continued to give a tenth of our income to God each week.

At the time, we had no plans for a house, and we didn't really have time to even look for one. But God had other plans! When Amy was 13 weeks pregnant, our pastor sent Amy a text message on a Monday: "House next door for sale." It had just gone on the market that day, so Amy and I decided to set up a viewing with the realtor for the following day. Our pastor talked with the people living in the house, and they agreed we could walk through that afternoon.

After work, we pulled up outside the two-story, plantation-style house. I looked at Amy and could tell she

# PAYCHECK TO PAYCHECK

was thinking the same thing as me. *We could never afford this home, but we're here.* I stepped out of the car still wearing my shirt and tie from work.

We walked in the front door. "I love the wood floors," Amy said. They stretched throughout the entire first floor. The living room had two huge windows and a fireplace. We walked up the stairs, looked at the master bedroom and started to see ourselves in the home. The next room had pink walls. "This is a princess room," Amy said. "I could see Brooke in this room."

"Look at this one," I called from the doorway. "Little Dom can have this room." She peeked into the room with white walls and nodded. In the next room, I pointed at the trophy shelves lining the walls. "Perfect for his baseball trophies!" I smiled.

We walked to the last room painted an earthy sage tone. "Perfect for the baby," Amy said as she rested her hand on her stomach. We didn't know if it was a boy or girl, so the neutral color was perfect.

We hadn't saved much, but we liked the house. "Let's try and get pre-approved and see what happens," I suggested. "It can't hurt to try." We didn't talk much about getting the house, but we prayed every day. Even so, I didn't think it would work out. In that market, sales were taking months and months. Bidding wars and a market flooded with foreclosures slowed the process — but not this time.

I prayed each day with Brooklynn as I drove her to preschool, and every night we remembered to thank God for our income. It was like God put each step in place and pushed any possible setbacks aside. This house wasn't a foreclosure. Somehow, even our money issues and credit history weren't a problem. We'd never been able to save, but this time, within two months, we had $15,000 to put down. I was astounded! We'd saved even while giving one-tenth to God. God did bless our 90 percent!

I stood in awe of what God accomplished. The 2,200-square-foot, two-story home with five bedrooms, three baths and a pool only cost $233,000, and we had $15,000 to put down. We saw the house for the first time on April 19, were in escrow a week later and exactly nine weeks later were moving in. Our pastor arranged to have a few guys from church empty our storage. To my surprise, they moved our belongings into our new home while I was at work. My living room was set up, and the kitchen was even stocked with a few groceries.

Before I released every area of my life to God, I lived paycheck to paycheck with nothing to show for it. Living my own way ruined my credit, cost me homes and almost cost me my family. I was an emotional wreck, riddled with guilt, overwhelmed with depression. I hated myself and even thought of suicide.

But now, Jesus offered me more than a new start; he offered me a whole new life. When I stopped trying to do everything my own way and released my life to God, for the first time in my life, I felt complete. Jesus was the missing piece I'd been searching for. I became a better husband, and little by little, my life and relationship with

# PAYCHECK TO PAYCHECK

Amy changed. I'm still learning and still make mistakes, but I'm moving forward all the time. I want to pass on what I've learned to my children and lead my family in the ways God desires.

Our pastor lives right next door. He's been a role model to me after not having a dad for so long. Just last night, I sat with my family in our family room where we have chosen not to have a TV to distract us from each other. I relaxed in our big brown chair in front of the warm fireplace with my Bible on my lap. Little Dom and Brooklynn made a bed out of blankets on the wood floor. As they snuggled between the blankets, baby Hank crawled around them. We talked about the Bible. Amy sat across the room doing homework at the dining table where she listened in. It was cozy.

I gazed at the decorative lettering we pasted on the wall above our sofa. The words are from Jeremiah 29:11 in the Bible. "'For I know the plans I have for you,' declares the LORD, 'plans to prosper you and not to harm you, plans to give you hope and a future.'"

I rest content, knowing God's plan is working out much better than my plan ever did.

# FULL CIRCLE
## THE STORY OF MARIELA
### WRITTEN BY KAREN KOCZWARA

"Your father is dead."

I stared at my grandfather, unable to believe his abrupt words. "Dead?" I'd just seen my father a few hours ago, smiling in his dapper blue suit. He was so excited about that helicopter ride. And now, just like that, he was dead? Gone?

"I'm afraid the weather was bad. They lost visibility, and the helicopter went down. He died instantly," my grandfather explained quietly. "I know what a shock this is."

I was speechless, my heart racing as the blue suit flashed again in my mind. My father was a pastor and a police officer — a pillar in the community. And, at home, a monster the world did not know. Was it wrong to feel relief? Was it wrong to be glad he would never hurt me again with his words or his hands? After all, he'd snatched me away from the person I loved most. Was it too much to hope that in the midst of this tragedy, I'd find her again?

☙☙☙

Most little girls want to walk in their mother's shadows at some point. They teeter in their mother's too-big high

# DEFYING CIRCUMSTANCE

heels when they try them on, twirl in the mirror in fancy dresses, smear lipstick on their tiny lips and dream about growing up to be just like Mommy one day. I was that little girl, always walking two steps behind my mother, her shadow my guide, her presence my safety. Until, one terrible day that was all taken away.

I was born in 1982, in Southern California. My biological father had four other children with another woman.

He walked away from my life when I was born, leaving my mother and me to navigate life on our own. As a young girl, I loved taking long walks with my mother, visiting the library with her and attending family functions together. Despite the struggles that came with being a single mother, she always did her best to ensure I was loved and cared for. A special bond grew between us, but when I was just 9 years old, my father came back into my life.

"Honey, I'm so sorry, but you're going to live with Daddy now," my mother said one day, tears streaming down her cheeks as she stooped down to hug me fiercely. "You know how much Mommy loves you, and that will never change."

I stared into her eyes, my own filled with fear. "But I don't want to live with him. I want to stay with you," I insisted, starting to cry. "Please, Mommy!"

"I know, I know, sweetie. I don't want it this way, either. But the judge says I don't have a choice. I'll get to visit you, though, I promise."

## FULL CIRCLE

"Will I have to go to a different school?" I asked through my tears.

My mother nodded sadly. "I'm afraid so. But you're such a nice girl, I'm sure you'll make new friends within no time!"

I didn't want to make new friends, I didn't want to go to a new school and I certainly didn't want to leave my mother. How could this be happening? It wasn't fair!

My mother tried to keep a brave face as she helped me pack my special things. I was too young to understand the injustices of life, too young to realize I'd been stolen from my mother in a terrible custody fight in which my father paid off a fellow police officer to gain full rights to a daughter he'd disowned. And just like that, I left my mother's arms, and my nightmare began.

I moved into my father's house with my new stepmother, Jean, her children and my father's children. I hated my stepmother from the very first day; she was cruel, living up to the "evil stepmother" cliché from the pages of fairy tale storybooks. "You stupid, fat pig! You better learn to clean up around here and start pulling your own weight!" she screamed at me. "You're just a useless nothing!"

I lay on my new bed at night, pulling the covers up to my chin as the tears came in a flood. This just wasn't fair! My heart ached, and I longed to be back under the safety and love of my mother. I thought of her sweet smile, the subtle scent of her skin, the favorite dishes she cooked in the kitchen late at night. She'd tried so hard to do everything right, and now she'd been ripped from my life, replaced by a monster I could not stand.

One day, as we played in the backyard, my stepmother's son hit my brother. "Hey, watch it!" I cried, lunging forward to push her son away. Later that night, my stepmother, who worked late nights at a car rental company, woke me in a rage.

"What the h*** were you thinking, hitting my son?" she screamed, yanking the covers off and slapping me in the face. "How dare you, you stupid pig! Don't you ever do that again!"

I cowered in the darkness, tears pricking my eyes as the shadow of her angry face hovered over me. I hated, *hated* her. I just wished she'd go away for good. "I'm sorry," I sputtered at last. "It won't happen again."

"D*** right it won't," she muttered, storming out of the room and slamming the door behind her.

I threw myself into school, trying to be the best student I could. School was my refuge, a place to escape the madness in my new home. I was shy and had a difficult time making new friends, but I convinced myself I didn't need any. Why bother getting close to people when they might be taken out of my life, too?

One day when I got home, my stepmother flew at me with fiery eyes. "What did you do with my black pants?" she demanded.

I stared at her. "I don't know what you're talking about. I haven't touched your black pants."

"Don't lie to me, you stupid girl!" she cried. "You

know d*** well you took my pants, and you better give them back, you little thief!"

"I swear, I never touched them," I insisted, shaking as I backed away from her. Why was she always so mean? I hadn't done anything to her!

"That girl is a thief, I swear!" I overheard my stepmother telling the family later that night. "Nothin' but a no-good, low-life thief, I tell you!"

Her words burned a mark on my soul. That night, I cried myself to sleep, praying that one day I would be reunited with my mother, back where I belonged.

The next morning, I saw my stepmother wearing her black pants. "You found them!" I said, relieved. Now she could no longer place the blame on me.

My stepmother shrugged but did not offer an apology as she brushed past me. Anger stirred inside me, but I bit my tongue to keep from lashing out. She'd already gotten after me for getting a B on my math test; I didn't need any more trouble around here.

In addition to owning his own security business, my father was a pastor at a local church. He took us to church each Sunday, seating us in front as he read from a big leather Bible at the pulpit. I loved the upbeat praise music, but it was difficult watching my father preach, as I knew a completely different man than the one in the suit and tie — a man even more frightening than my stepmother.

"Here, boys, go down to the store for me," my father said one night, tossing a few crumpled dollar bills at my stepbrothers. "Go on, now."

## DEFYING CIRCUMSTANCE

As the boys obediently filed out the door, my heart began to race; I knew the drill all too well. With the house empty, my father could now take advantage of me. He walked me into my room, shut the door and molested me. "Here, now, don't you tell anyone, you hear?" he threatened, shoving a few bucks in my hand. "This is just between us, you got it?"

As his eyes bore into mine, I nodded meekly. "Yes, sir," I said quietly. "I won't tell anyone." The minute he left the room, I crawled under the covers and cried, feeling dirty and ashamed and all alone. Why had my father taken me away from my mother only to abuse me? I didn't belong here! I missed my mother, and I wanted to go home.

My stepmother eventually moved out of the house, but my father's abuse continued. I felt sick as the church members filed by him on Sunday, calling out cheerful hellos. "Great message, Pastor!" they said. "See you next week!"

"God bless you!" my father returned with a smile.

*If only they knew,* I thought, my stomach twisting. *What a hypocrite!* I'd thought about reporting his abuse, but judging by their ignorant smiles, I feared no one would believe me if I told the truth. And so I kept my terrible secret to myself.

Though my mother was supposed to receive visitation, my father prevented this from happening by playing evil tricks. One day, when my mother was supposed to pick me up from school, my father came early for me. "I thought my mother was picking me up," I said with disappointment as I got in the car. I'd been looking forward to her visit like it was Christmastime.

"She couldn't make it," he said coolly, revving the engine. "Sorry, kid."

My heart sank. Later, I learned my mother did indeed show up at the school, but we were already gone. My father told the courts she was a no-show.

One afternoon, I met my father at the mailbox. As he sifted through the stack of envelopes, a letter slipped from his hands. "What's this?" I asked, grabbing it. Immediately, I recognized my mother's beautiful handwriting. "This is from my mother!" I gasped.

"Gimme that," my father snapped, snatching it from my hands. "That's just garbage, Mariela."

"How many other letters has she written me?" I demanded, growing angry. "Have you just been throwing them away?!"

"You live with me now, kid, remember? Your mother has a new life now," my father snapped, brushing past me and into the house.

I ran to my room, ripped open the envelope and read my mother's precious words. "How are you, sweetie? I miss you so much. I pray every day we can be together again," she wrote. My tears spilled onto the paper as I gently slipped it back into the envelope.

"Oh, Mom," I whispered into the stillness of my room. "I miss you, too."

Though I was relieved my stepmother was gone, I was

still sickened by my father's presence and the abuse that continued. One night, as I lay in bed, I cried out to God. "Please, please, let me see my mother again! Please!" As the tears spilled down my cheeks, I thought about the God my father preached about on Sundays. He sounded like a loving God, a God who cared about our needs, a God we could call out to in times of trouble. Was it possible he heard the desperate prayers of a little girl?

As I huddled under the covers, I suddenly saw a bright light coming through the three little windows to my left. I sat up in bed and stared outside, shocked at what I saw. Though I could not make out any distinct features, I was sure of one thing: I had seen an angel! As the bright light faded into the distance, I lay back down, a new warmth forming in my heart. Despite my heartache and seemingly bleak situation, I was now sure that somehow everything was going to be okay. God would get me out of this place one day.

My stepmother drifted in and out of our lives, while my father began dating other women. One Sunday, in early January 1995, my father announced he was going on a date with his new girlfriend. "How do I look?" he asked, emerging from the bedroom in a sharp-looking blue suit and a boutonniere tucked into his lapel.

"Fine," I mumbled. "Where are you going all dressed up?"

He beamed. "I'm surprising my girlfriend by taking her on a helicopter ride. I think she's just going to love it!"

"Where am I going to go?" I asked.

# FULL CIRCLE

"I'm taking you to Jean's house. You will go to church with her," he said.

I didn't want to see Jean, and I didn't really want to go to church, but I obeyed and trudged off to put on my best Sunday clothes. A couple hours later, as I sat in church, the sun streaming through the windows, I felt a tap on my shoulder. "Mariela, I need to talk to you outside," my grandfather whispered. Where had he come from, and why was he interrupting the service to talk to me?

I followed him outside. His eyes were serious as they met mine. "Mariela, if something were to happen to your father, who would you want to live with? Me or Jean?" he asked.

I blinked, taken aback by his question. "I'd want to live with my mother," I replied hastily. "Why are you asking?"

My grandfather took a deep breath. "Your father was killed in a helicopter crash this morning," he said slowly. "It's all over the news. Terrible tragedy. I'm so sorry, kid."

My father was dead? I could hardly believe it. A mixture of relief and sadness washed over me as I thought about my father, so dapper in his blue suit, boasting about his special date just hours before. "What happened?" I asked with wide eyes.

"The police are still piecing the details together, but it appears the helicopter got tangled up in some telephone wires just over the Coalinga Pass, and it crashed. Your father's girlfriend is in critical condition but survived. Why don't you come with me until we can sort this all out?"

## DEFYING CIRCUMSTANCE

My grandfather gently tugged at my hand, and I followed him in a daze.

*Dead*. I tried to process the news. The man would never hurt me again; he was gone for good. Was it possible that God had really answered my prayers by taking him out of my life? Would I now be able to live with my mother again? My heart soared at the thought of being reunited with her, but I knew the next few weeks would be nothing short of a living hell.

The days before my father's funeral were a blur of activity and confusion. Suddenly, family members I hadn't even known about popped up out of nowhere to express their condolences.

Their ulterior motives were soon exposed; a large life insurance policy was at stake, and everyone wanted his or her hands on that money.

On the day of my father's funeral, I donned my nicest black dress and followed the sea of mourners into the church to remember my father. As a well-known businessman and pastor, my father had accumulated many acquaintances over the years. More than 3,000 people attended his service, including the entire San Bernardino police force and the entire church where he'd pastored. I had never seen so many people in one place at one time.

I sat numbly in my seat as fellow members of the church and community spoke about my father. "He was a good man, an honorable man," one person began. I stared at the ground, trying to tune the words out. The smiling,

## FULL CIRCLE

sociable man the world knew and loved was certainly not the man I knew.

"Your father was a wonderful man," a woman said to me as she filed out of the church. "I'm so sorry for your loss."

"Yes, he will be missed," I mumbled, forcing a sad smile. *Missed by you, but certainly not by me,* I thought to myself, shaking my head. I could hardly wait to move on from this chaos and begin the next chapter of my life.

To my utter relief and joy, the courts granted me the life insurance money and agreed I should be reunited with my mother. When I fell back into her arms, I was filled with such happiness I could scarcely breathe. Her sweet scent was just the same, the fine lines around her eyes still there, her smile just as I remembered it. I was 13 now and quite a different girl than I was when I'd been snatched from her arms four years ago. Life had beaten me up, and I no longer possessed the innocence I'd once had. But I was thankful to be home at last, back where I belonged.

My mother and I spent several months catching up, swapping stories, laughs and many hugs. Though I loved being in her presence, my heart had hardened, and I soon became enticed by the exciting things of the world. That summer, I met my first boyfriend. He was 18, and I was flattered by his attention. Not long into our relationship, he pressured me to have sex, and I relented. A piece of my soul had already been taken away years before; what did it matter now?

One day, my mother walked into the kitchen with my

diary in her hands. "Do you want to explain this?" she demanded, her eyes sad.

"Why are you reading that?" I cried, grabbing it out of her hands. "That's private!"

"You're sleeping with your boyfriend?" she asked, shaking her head. "Really, Mariela, I'm disappointed in you. You're way too young for this sort of behavior. You tell that boyfriend of yours goodbye. You are not to see him again."

I burst into tears. "I'm so sorry, Mom," I cried. "It just … happened."

"It may have just happened, but it won't happen again," she insisted.

We relocated to Monterey that summer. Though I loved the beautiful beach and cool morning fog that rolled in over the hills, I detested having to start all over again at a new school. I was still painfully shy and had a tough time meeting others. At last, I made friends with a girl in my ninth grade class, and we began hanging out. One night, her brother enticed me into his bedroom, and I gave in. I remembered my mother's words of warning, but it seemed the only way to keep a guy around was to surrender to his wishes.

One chilly October day, I discovered, to my horror, that I was pregnant. As I stared at the little white stick in my hands, I shook my head in disbelief. I was only 14; how could this happen? I told my friend's brother right away.

"Look, no one can know about this," he hissed. He had a girlfriend and had just been using me on the side. "I'll take care of it, okay? You just gotta get rid of it." A few days later, he handed me a wad of cash. "You're gonna take care of it, right?"

I nodded numbly. "Yeah." I made an appointment at a local clinic and had an abortion. *I'm too young to be a mother,* I convinced myself as the technician performed the procedure. But the pain that stung my insides matched the pain in my heart as I drove home that afternoon.

The next day at school, my friend confronted me. "You sleepin' with my brother?" she demanded, getting into my face.

"What I do is none of your business," I replied, squirming away from her angry stare.

"Oh, really? That's my brother we're talkin' about! Is that why you're friends with me? To get to him? Who else you sleepin' with around school?"

"No one!" I cried, jumping back. "Leave me alone!"

"You're sleepin' around, aren't you? You little slut!"

"You calling me a slut?" I lost control and threw a punch at my friend. She fought back, and we wrestled each other to the ground, pulling hair and cursing until the principal finally pulled us apart. I stormed away, angry with myself for losing control and angry with my friend for accusing me with harsh words. I decided I'd just keep to myself, be a loner and leave everyone alone. I didn't need *anyone*!

During the following year, I dodged the social scene, choosing to focus on my studies instead. When the high school dances rolled around, I didn't dare show up. Soon, rumors about me began to swirl around campus; some kids said I was stuck up. At last, fed up with my reputation, I decided to give in and join the fun. It seemed all the cool kids smoked, drank and slept around. If that was the way to gain popularity, I'd just have to do those things, too.

My older brother was popular and knew where all the parties were on Friday night. "You should come with me next week," he suggested. "I can introduce you to everyone."

"Sure," I agreed. At last, here was my chance to break out of my shell.

When Friday night arrived, my brother made a stop at the liquor store. "Just follow me, and keep quiet," he instructed as we went inside.

I strode behind him, imitating his casual stance as he browsed the aisles. When he grabbed a bottle of tequila off the shelf, he glanced at me and quickly ducked out the door. "I can't believe you stole that so easily!" I said, giggling when we got back into the car.

"I do it all the time," he confessed. "A lot easier to steal a big bottle of booze than a case of beer, so I stick to the hard stuff."

The music was pumping and the beer was flowing when we arrived at the party. "You smoke?" a guy asked, pulling me aside.

I shrugged. "Sometimes," I lied.

"I don't mean cigarettes," he said, giving me a knowing glance.

# FULL CIRCLE

"Oh." I knew most of the kids at my school smoked pot. I'd never tried it before but figured there was a first time for everything.

The first time I smoked a joint, my lungs burned, and I thought I was going to throw up. But the more I smoked it, the more I liked it. It made me feel silly and happy and helped me ease out of my shy exterior. Before long, smoking and drinking were a regular part of my weekend. With the partying came the guys, and I soon became sexually active again. Slowly, the remains of my tender heart from the past slipped away as I gave myself to a world I hoped would accept me.

In 2000, I graduated high school. I was partly relieved that these days were behind me but also had no idea what my future held. I met a new guy, and we began hanging out. In April 2001, I learned I was pregnant again. This time, I wanted to keep the baby. I told my boyfriend, who said adamantly, "I grew up without a father, and I won't do that to my child. I'm gonna make sure my child knows me."

I was happy he wasn't planning to leave and even happier when he suggested we get married the following month. We wed in a simple ceremony. I was just 18, technically an adult, but still with so much to learn. My new husband got laid off from his job as a custodian for the school district and began selling drugs full time to make a living. I wasn't thrilled about his choice, but with a new baby on the way, I figured any sort of income was better than none.

## DEFYING CIRCUMSTANCE

In December 2001, I gave birth to a beautiful little girl, Nora. I was ecstatic to be a mother and determined that nothing would tear our family apart. The memory of my childhood was still fresh in my mind, and I wanted my daughter to have two loving parents in her life as she grew up.

We moved into a house on an old military base, and my husband's new "business" began to thrive. He purchased new cars, bought our daughter the finest clothes and made sure I was always well taken care of. Cocaine was the drug of choice in our part of town, and my husband was the go-to guy. I continued smoking pot and went back to work when Nora was just a few months old. I convinced myself that we lived a normal, happy life, but our world was just about to get turned upside down.

One day, I came home from work to find cops swarming around our house. "Where's my husband?" I asked frantically, running toward the house. "What's going on?"

"Your husband's been taken into custody," a police officer explained. "You can't go into the house right now."

My heart sank; he'd finally been caught. Just last week, I'd asked him if he was being careful. "The cops aren't stupid," I reminded him. "You lose your job, and then you're driving around in flashy cars and wearing nice clothes. You think they aren't going to catch on to you?"

"I've been selling since I was 13," my husband drawled. "I know what I'm doing, Mariela. Trust me."

But now, it had all caught up to him. I was devastated.

# FULL CIRCLE

I soon learned the full story. Just as I'd suspected, the cops had been building up a case on him for some time. When they finally felt they had sufficient evidence, they sent in an undercover cop, who busted him on the spot. Because we lived on federal property, the courts had to abide by certain federal regulations. They sentenced my husband to nine years in prison on multiple counts of drug possession and sales. My life as I knew it had come to an end.

"I'm so sorry, baby," my husband said, kissing Nora and me as he prepared to leave for a prison in San Jose. "I don't want our baby daughter to forget me. Please come visit me as often as you can."

"I will," I promised. "I'll visit every weekend."

I kept my promise, making the hour-and-a-half drive north every weekend before the sun came up. Because the visitations were first come first serve, I was forced to stand in line at 4 a.m. along with a sea of other women waiting to visit their guys. I bundled Nora in tiny little sweaters and shivered as the wind whipped at my cheeks. This certainly wasn't how I'd envisioned my first year of marriage would be.

My husband was transferred to a prison in New Jersey, and I still got on that plane to see him. He made several collect phone calls a day, racking up our phone bill. I grew resentful and wondered what sort of life our daughter would have. Though I pondered divorce, I felt in my heart that God would be angry with me if I left him. *Besides, he's my soul mate,* I convinced myself.

"Look, Nora, there's Daddy," I said to my little girl,

pointing to a picture of my husband before I put her down for bed. "Daddy," I repeated.

Her eyes grew wide, and she clapped her chubby hands. I was thankful for the wonderful gift of my daughter but not sure how much longer I could go on living alone. Our bills were piling up, we had next to nothing in the cupboards and I hardly had enough money to fill my car with gas. I needed a husband who would provide for me, but instead he'd left me in the lurch.

My mother, always one to look after me, used her beautiful house in Monterey to secure bail to get my husband out of jail.

"I can't stand to see you living this way, baby," she said wearily. "You and your husband belong together. Nora needs him."

My husband returned home for four months on bail. During this time, he cheated on me with another woman. I was furious. "How could you do that to me after everything I've done for you?" I cried.

"I'm sorry, it won't happen again," he assured me. "I'm really sorry, Mariela."

I wasn't sure if I believed him. A few weeks later, when I caught him with the other woman, my rage escalated to a new level. When I saw the woman riding home on her bike, I got into my car, stepped on the gas and chased after her. Just as she turned the corner, I veered to the side of the road and hit the back wheel of her bike. She went flying to the ground, and immediately I knew I was in trouble.

# FULL CIRCLE

The woman called the cops, but they didn't come for me until the following year. Just when I thought all had been forgotten, a cop came to my door one day with a warrant for my arrest. The cop later explained that they'd gotten my case entangled with a similar one, which had caused the delay. In court, I faced up to 43 years in prison for attempted assault. I thought of Nora, my precious daughter, back home. With my husband fresh out of jail and now my arrest, I risked losing my child. I had to fight back.

By a miracle, my sentence was reduced to a mere four months of house arrest. I was elated. My daughter would not be taken from me! Years later I would understand that someone had been looking out for me, and I'd learn the true definition of mercy and grace.

In August 2007, my husband got transferred to a Colorado prison. I left my job, picked up everything and moved to Colorado to be closer to him. I hoped our move to a new state might be a clean slate for us, but instead, our marriage only grew worse.

My husband became verbally abusive and had other women visit him regularly in prison. Angry and alone, I decided to indulge in partying as he had done. I began drinking again, this time more heavily, and going to clubs. One night when I was out, I met a cute guy.

"I should let you know I'm married," I said upfront as we chatted over a drink.

"I'm just getting out of a 15-year marriage myself," he said. "I've been separated from my wife after she cheated on me." He went on to explain how difficult his life had been the past few years, and I resonated with his pain. By the time the night was over, I felt myself falling for him.

The following year, I moved back to California and filed for divorce. I'd had enough of the lying, the cheating, the abuse and the negligence. My new boyfriend left his wife for good, and we began a new life together. He showed me a love and respect I'd never experienced before, and for the first time, I learned what it felt like to be treated like a woman.

After just six months of dating, I learned I was pregnant. "Let's get married," my boyfriend said eagerly. "I love you, Mariela, and I want to love your daughter and raise our new baby together with you."

I was ecstatic. At last, I had found true love. In August 2008, we moved back to Southern California, and in February of the following year, my second daughter, Lilly, was born. She was an exceptionally happy baby, and I instantly fell in love. In September that year, my boyfriend and I were married. I continued smoking pot and drinking, and my new husband smoked cigarettes. I thought many times about quitting but didn't know how in the world I'd ever muster the strength. I'd smoked pot since I was a teenager, and my entire extended family drank and smoked. How could I ever break free of my destructive ways?

On New Year's Day 2010, I made a New Year's resolution to stop smoking pot. "God can help you stop, Mariela," my husband reminded me.

# FULL CIRCLE

I wondered if this could be true. I'd tried so many times to quit, but I couldn't imagine not being high. What would I do if I had to face myself completely sober? Would I even like the girl in the mirror?

Two weeks later, my husband went to the doctor with what he thought was an infection. "Your lymph nodes are extremely enlarged, but I think a strong round of antibiotics should do the trick," the doctor said.

But when his symptoms worsened, I became concerned. He grew extremely fatigued and experienced terrible headaches. "I think you should go back to the doctor," I urged him.

"Wow, your lymph nodes are really enlarged," the nurse observed when we returned to the doctor's office. "You need to go to the emergency room right away."

"That can't be good," I whispered to my husband as we sped off to the hospital. We had both discussed the possibility of cancer; his father had died of lung cancer, and we knew he was at risk. Still, I refused to believe it until we heard the words.

The diagnosis at the emergency room confirmed my worst fear. My husband had Hodgkin's Lymphoma. "I think we've caught it early enough, but we're still going to need to go through chemotherapy," the doctor said.

I surprised both the doctors and myself by remaining calm. Though God and I hadn't spoken in some time, I suddenly felt a peace and comfort that I was certain could only come from him. Somehow, in that moment, I knew we were all going to be okay. My husband and I walked outside, and he pulled a cigarette out of his pocket. "This is going to be my very last one," he said. "And I mean it this time."

We leaned against the building and smoked one last cigarette together. "Are you scared?" I asked, taking a drag.

He shook his head. "No. God told me not long ago that if I did have cancer, it wouldn't kill me. I know it's going to be hard on us both, but I'm going to pull through this."

"I know you are," I said, taking his hand. As I snuffed out the last of the cigarette, another wave of that unexplainable peace washed over me. We strode back inside, and the doctors admitted my husband for the next three days until the final biopsy results came back.

I thought long and hard about my life over the next several days. I had spent most of my life running from God, afraid that if I got too close to him, he'd leave me or hurt me like nearly everyone else in my life had. Yet, despite the many years that had passed, I never forgot about him. Now, facing my biggest challenge yet, I realized I didn't want to do it alone. I needed the strength that could only come from him, the peace that only he could provide. And more importantly, I needed to know that when I died, I would go to be with him in heaven. The diagnosis reminded me that life was precious, and I did not want to spend the rest of my life wondering if I'd spend eternity with God.

I looked up churches in our area and found one right near our house. The very next Sunday, we attended Colton

# FULL CIRCLE

First Assembly of God together. As I sat in my seat, tears spilled down my cheeks, and my heart was softened like never before. The peace I'd experienced in the hospital came over me again, and despite the uncertainty that lay before me, I felt more hope than I had in years. "The things of your past stop here," I felt God tell me. "Your chains have been broken."

Right then and there, I gave my life over to God. "I know I've done many bad things in my past, but please make me new right now," I prayed. "I want to live my life going forward with you. I know I can't break free of my bad habits without your strength, so please help me. Thank you for loving me and for not giving up on me."

I took a deep breath as I opened my eyes. It felt as if a weight I'd been dragging around my whole life had finally been lifted off my back. I had God on my side! As the pastor said, God was not concerned with my past. He only cared about my heart now. I could rest knowing he would carry me through life's struggles and heartaches and give me the strength to face each new day.

The next few months were difficult as I watched my husband undergo intensive chemotherapy. His red blood cells plummeted, and I had to inject him with medicine to boost his immunity. I'd never been fond of needles, but with God's strength, I remained calm and supportive. To both of our surprise, my husband experienced odd side effects from the treatment. While most chemotherapy patients lose hair and weight, my husband began to gain weight, his slender 150-pound frame plumping to a healthy 175 pounds. His hair also grew thicker than ever before, and we both laughed at the "new man" he'd become.

"Wow, you look better than ever!" I said one day. "For a moment there, I forgot you had cancer," I added teasingly.

My husband took my hand. "Thank you, Mariela. I don't know what I'd do without you. We're going to get through this together." Though he had always loved God, the many trials of his life had beaten him down over the years. But he had always remained an encouragement to me, and during this difficult time, he surrendered his whole heart to God. I was so thankful we were united not only spiritually, but in life as well. Some might have said fate brought us together, but I knew better. God was the one working behind the scenes, and his plan was greater than mine.

"God, I really need your help to stop smoking pot," I continued to pray. "I know I can't do this alone." I'd been smoking for so long, I feared I'd hardly recognize myself if I wasn't high. I'd always felt pot made life more enjoyable; things were funnier and more lighthearted after a few joints. But I knew God wanted not only my whole heart, but my whole being as well, and this included all my habits, good and bad. It was time to surrender the pot once and for all.

To my surprise, I liked the new me. When I quit smoking pot, I had a clear mind and could focus on things that really mattered, like supporting my husband and

# FULL CIRCLE

spending time with my girls. I thanked God for helping me to stay strong, and to my delight, I had no urge to return to my old ways. My old friend pot was a thing of the past.

Our faith was put to the test again in July 2010. My husband's unemployment benefits ended, and we could not afford our next month's rent. I applied for a job as a property manager at a public storage facility. Not only did I get the job, but it came with a bonus: Our family could live rent and utilities free in the large two-bedroom apartment upstairs!

"I can't believe how good God is!" I said to my husband. "Look at this place! A laundry room, two huge bedrooms and it's just down the street from our new church! I don't know what more I could ask for."

Two months later, my husband was declared cancer free. We praised God for his amazing provision and healing.

I wondered how on earth I would have survived the past year of my life without God. He had truly brought us to our knees, causing us to rely on him every step of the way. The journey had been difficult, but we could now see the sunlight through the clouds.

Everything, from the TV shows we watched to the way we talked to the music we listened to, changed in our home when we invited God into our lives. My whole life, I'd had a rather sassy, critical attitude, but now, as a follower of God, I wanted to represent him well. I tried to watch my every word, speaking kindly to people and offering words of encouragement instead of tearing them down. My sailor mouth disappeared, too.

"I can't remember the last time you lost your temper," my husband mused one day. "Who is this new woman of mine, and what has she done with my wife?"

I laughed. "Don't plan on ever seeing that other woman again," I replied.

My mother moved in with us, and I encouraged her to stop drinking. "If God can help me get sober, he can help you, too," I told her. "You just have to call on him for strength."

As my mother watched my words turn into actions, her heart slowly turned, and she eventually gave up the bottle for good. I praised God for using me in her life and hoped I could encourage many more people who struggled with addiction.

My husband and I got more involved at our wonderful church, Colton First Assembly of God. I began teaching the girls' class and considered it a privilege to work with the children.

Since I was a young girl, I'd always had a desire to work with children someday, and God had finally fulfilled that. My husband began ushering and working with the high school students, and together we enrolled in a class where we learned more about God.

One day after church, I shared a Bible verse with my husband. "Listen to this. It says in Matthew 6:33: 'But seek first his kingdom and his righteousness and all these things will be given to you as well.' I thought it would be so hard to give up my old ways, but instead, when I began seeking God's kingdom, I found more fulfillment than I ever did in my past. I can't believe how much he's blessed us. I never dreamed I'd be living a life like this."

"God is really good," my husband agreed. "He gave me my physical life back, but more importantly, a new life with him."

But there was still something else I had to do, something that had been tugging at my heart for some time.

As I read my Bible and thanked God for forgiving me of my past wrongdoings, I realized that I needed to forgive those who had hurt me, too. My father was long gone, and I had forgiven him in my heart, but there was still someone else I needed to make things right with.

I took a deep breath, picked up the phone and made the call. "This is Mariela," I stammered when my stepmother answered. "Do you have a minute?"

"Mariela! What a surprise to hear from you!"

We talked for some time, and I told her that I had forgiven her for the pain she'd caused me all those years ago. "I hope you will forgive me, too, for holding a grudge against you," I added.

"Oh, Mariela, of course I do. And I'm so sorry. I may not have shown it, but I always thought of you as one of my own. I'm so glad you called."

Relief washed over me as I hung up the phone. I thanked God for giving me the strength to do the right thing.

**DEFYING CIRCUMSTANCE**

The girl of my youth — rejected, hurt and abused — was a distant memory, replaced by a woman of confidence, strength and joy. God had truly brought my life full circle.

# SLAYING THE THREE-HEADED MONSTER
## THE STORY OF JOSÉ
### WRITTEN BY JESSICA BOLING

Sweat oozed from my pores, soaking the sheets above and beneath me. I reached to wipe my forehead. My hand shook so much that I slapped myself in the face. Suddenly, violently, my whole body jerked. The bed shook.

I lay alone. I was alone. No one could reach through the dark fog of my mind. My mother had tried. My wife had tried. Other people had, too, but drugs and drinks were my only companions. They held me, both brain and body, in their vice-like grip. Marijuana, cocaine and alcohol comprised a three-headed monster that took another bite of my life every day.

"I won't do it again!" My voice quavered, shook and broke, cutting through the dark room like a sharp knife. "No more drugs. I'm going to stop."

Finally, my body lapsed into a stupor-like sleep. Only a few hours later, I woke up to broad daylight pouring through the bedroom window. I didn't think about my words in the night. The monster was attacking me again. All I could think about was getting more drugs into my body. I rolled out of bed and crossed the room, grabbing a table for support. On the table lay a small plastic bag filled with coarse white powder. Eagerly, still shaking a little and feeling my muscles tighten with anxiety, I poured a little of the powder onto my hand and snorted it.

# DEFYING CIRCUMSTANCE

Almost immediately, I felt the relief. Energy surged through my body, dispelling the exhaustion and unsteadiness. I felt like I could conquer the world. For a few moments, I believed that everything was fine — that my life was good. But the feeling didn't last. As soon as it waned, I snorted more cocaine, drank more beer and smoked more pot. The cycle seemed endless, and I could barely remember what my life was like before it began.

❧❧❧

I grew up in Compton, California, a suburb of Los Angeles. Compton was infamous for its high murder and drug rates. Drug dealers pushed their wares to anyone who approached them.

My parents hated the culture of drugs and crime and made every effort to keep us away from it. Dad and Mom worked hard to send us to a private school. I attended Verbum Dei, a Catholic all-male high school, in the early 1970s.

Although Verbum Dei boasted a nicer campus and a higher quality education than the area's public schools, the surrounding culture of drugs and violence still lurked within its borders.

One day my father drove up to the school building and found me sitting on the front steps with a group of guys. Each of the other teenagers wore something red — a shirt, a bandana or a belt. Dad eyed them with suspicion as he called me to the car.

## SLAYING THE THREE-HEADED MONSTER

I left my group and opened the passenger door.

"Who are those boys?" asked Dad.

I closed the door. "Friends."

Slowly, he drove away from the school. I glanced back toward the group and saw one of them make a hand gesture.

"You won't spend any more time with them." Dad's voice was firm, unemotional.

"Why not?"

"I won't let you become one of them." I saw Dad's jaw muscles tighten. "You will not join a gang."

I didn't answer.

A few weeks later, I went out after school with a group of friends. We went to a bar, and I drank too much. While walking the streets afterward, we stopped so one of the guys could paint some graffiti. Through vision blurred by alcohol, I saw my dad's thin body and flashing eyes.

"You're going home, José," he said. "Now."

"Where did you come from?" I asked.

Before my friends had a chance to respond, Dad seized my arm and guided me across the street and into his waiting car. Bewildered, upset, I clenched my fists and refused to look at my friends. Dad stared straight ahead as he drove home.

I was humiliated, but I had to respect my dad. The same scenario happened over and over during high school. Against my will, Dad protected me from joining a gang.

But I found other ways to rebel. In 1972, when I was a

# DEFYING CIRCUMSTANCE

sophomore, my girlfriend got pregnant. I became a father at age 16. My girlfriend and I married in 1973, and instead of dropping out of high school, I worked hard to graduate from Verbum Dei in 1974.

For a while, I worked to make our lives better. I spent nine months at a trade school in Arizona, studying technology, then returned to Los Angeles. Then one day in 1975, I was on a motorcycle with a friend when I saw a car merging into our lane. Before either of us could react, it struck us.

The high-speed impact knocked me off the motorcycle and sent me flying through the air. I landed 171 feet away in some bushes by the side of the highway.

Police sirens screamed. When the officers arrived, they cordoned off the area of the crash and searched, to no avail.

"There were two guys on the bike!" a bystander told the police.

"We can't find the other one," said one officer to the other. They had already taken my injured friend away in an ambulance.

"What about over there?" Another officer pointed to a patch of brush. "We can't see what's in those bushes."

The first two officers shook their heads. "He couldn't have been knocked that far."

"It's worth a look."

Finally, they searched the patch of brush and found me lying there. Medics rushed to place me on a gurney and get me to a waiting ambulance.

## SLAYING THE THREE-HEADED MONSTER

I woke up in the hospital. The pain was intense, and I was barely able to move. I glanced downward and saw that I was bandaged from my head to my knees. My chest ached with every breath, and the intense pain brought me nearly to tears.

"Doctor," I murmured the next time a white-coated man entered the room.

The doctor urged me not to speak. He said, "You are a lucky man. You have a dislocated hip and collarbone, which we have reset, but they will remain sore. There were a few broken ribs, a collapsed lung and some head trauma. Please rest as much as you can."

I was amazed that I had survived. My mother came to visit me, clutching her string of rosary beads in one hand. She leaned over my face, her dark eyes full of tears, and kissed my cheek.

"You will be well again, my José!" she said. "The doctor wouldn't even give me a 50 percent chance that you would survive. He said it was impossible to know since you were knocked unconscious. But I prayed." She held up her rosary beads and smiled again. "And now I know you will live."

My recovery was slow. For about six months, I walked with the help of a cane. Intense pain in my chest and hips persisted, but the doctor gave me medication to manage it. When my prescription ran out, I sought pain relief on the streets and in bars. When my bones ached, I drank or smoked pot to numb the pain. The more I drank and smoked, the more I craved. Over time, the addictions spiraled out of control, and I became part of the street drug culture in Compton.

After the accident, it was difficult to find work that I could physically do. I worked for short periods of time, mostly odd jobs — just enough to keep some money in my pocket. And just enough to feed my new addictions.

1976 found me in the midst of a divorce. The separation threw me into a deeper depression. I realized I'd never had a childhood. Throughout my teenage years I'd worked, trying to save money to support the child I fathered at age 16. It felt cruel and unfair. I'd been cheated out of a carefree adolescence. The more I thought about it, the more I drank and did drugs, trying to quell the tide of depression.

After the divorce, I went to live with my mother. She sat down next to me on the couch one day as I reclined, half drunk, watching television.

"José," she said. Her small, strong hand gripped mine, and she reached the other hand to pull my face toward her. I looked into her eyes, dark and determined, and knew she was serious about something.

"What is it?" I asked impatiently, trying to turn away.

She wouldn't let me. "José, you are throwing your life away. It is not trash!"

I shook my head. "What do you want?" I asked again, ignoring her statement.

"Remember your uncles?"

"Yes, I remember." Two of my uncles had died after overdosing on heroin.

## SLAYING THE THREE-HEADED MONSTER

"They threw their lives away. All the drugs are bad, but they took heroin, and it killed them." She leaned forward. I could feel her breath, warm and damp, in my ear. "José, I heard that you're taking heroin."

I turned to look her in the eyes. "No, I'm not."

She smiled and took a breath. I could never lie to her, and she knew it.

"I'm glad. I want you to promise me never to take it."

"I promise." I said it to satisfy her.

She pulled me close to her, and I knew she believed my promise. "I will trust you with this. And I will keep praying for you."

She rose and left the room, but the promise never left my mind. Although I'd made the promise to please her, I knew I couldn't break it. I loved her too much. And, I remembered seeing my two uncles descend into the ravages of heroin addiction, never to emerge alive.

Still, I lacked the courage to make sound decisions. I allowed drugs and alcohol to control my life. Around 1977, I met my future wife. We had a solid relationship, but she had to put up with a lot.

That same year, I got a job at a Ford Motor Company plant. My father put in a good word and landed me the position, but he felt uneasy about the atmosphere.

"It's a bad place for drugs," he said. "I want you to work, José, and this is a fine job, but many of the other workers are addicts."

I shrugged off his concern. "Don't worry, Dad. This is the perfect job for me."

## DEFYING CIRCUMSTANCE

Dad's concerns were legitimate. After only a few days on the job, I discovered the undercurrent of drug dealing and abuse that hummed alongside the car assembly lines at the Ford plant. I rode in each morning with Dad, who also worked at the plant, but during breaks I'd sneak away.

"Hey, José!" hissed Raul, one of my co-workers, as I walked down a hall during lunch break. "Want a joint?"

I glanced over my shoulder to ensure that Dad wasn't nearby. Then I smiled. "Yep."

Raul handed me a freshly rolled paper filled with marijuana. Together we slipped outside and climbed the narrow fire escape stairway to the roof. On the roof, gravel crunched beneath our feet. We trekked to the center of the roof, where no one below could catch a glimpse of us, and smoked.

My nostrils and lungs filled with the strong, sweet scent of marijuana, and I relaxed. Satisfied, I threw down the butt and smothered the embers with my shoe.

"Time to get back to work." Raul rose to his feet.

"Thanks, bro," I said. For the moment I was content, but in an hour I wanted more. Everything about the marijuana enticed me: the warmth of the smoke and embers, the sweetness of the smell and the calmness I felt after smoking a joint.

Dad eyed me with distrust as I got into his car and rode home, smelling of the weed I'd smoked. He knew what I was doing, but he couldn't control my decisions.

My wife couldn't change me, either. She accepted me, addictions and all, and we got married in 1983. By then,

## SLAYING THE THREE-HEADED MONSTER

addiction had closed its hand around my throat, and it held on with a vice-like grip.

☙☙☙☙

"You got some?" A shabbily dressed man crossed the sidewalk and slipped into the alley where I stood.

"Yeah," I said, reaching into my coat pocket. I brought out a packet of white powder, but when the man reached to touch it, I pulled back. "No, you have to pay first."

"How much?" he asked, reaching into his pocket.

I looked around. There were no cops in sight, but it was better to be safe than sorry. I moved farther into the darkness of the alley, gesturing for the man to follow.

We carried out the deal in semidarkness beneath the shadow of an adjacent building. The narrow passage smelled of urine and rotting food.

"Thanks, man." The man walked away with the packet of powder, and I recounted the stack of bills before shoving them in my pocket.

Despite my secretiveness, everyone knew I was a dealer. By 1986, I had a total of eight children. Their school friends laughed and teased them, saying, "Your dad's a drug dealer!"

I knew my children were ashamed of me. My wife held our family together, but it was difficult. She worried about me. She cared about me. I thought I cared about her and our children, but my decisions said that I cared only for myself. Above my kids, above my wife, I cared most about feeling good — about getting high and masking all the pain. I lived from one day to the next without any emotions except those affected by the drugs. I managed to get and sell more cocaine than I could use, dealing in back alleys to pick up some cash. It was an easy way to make money, especially because I couldn't hold down any other type of job.

In 1986, tired of the constant drug dealing and wanting to make a renewed effort to provide for my family, I managed to get a job at the local post office. They didn't run a drug test, or they would have turned me away.

After I'd worked at the post office for several months, my boss called me into his office. "Take a seat," he said.

I sat across from him at a wooden desk strewn with papers. He took a deep breath and shook his head. "José, you've been late to work four out of five days this week."

I swallowed and lowered my eyes.

"That is a problem, but we found a bigger problem today. You were smoking pot outside the back door during a break."

I nodded. It was true.

"I'm sorry, José. I hate to do this, but there's no other choice. I have to let you go." He reached into the desk drawer and drew out a folded paper. "Here's some information about a drug recovery program. If you complete the program, there's a chance you can come back. Think about it."

Still silent, I nodded again. There was nothing to say, so I took the paper and left the room.

## SLAYING THE THREE-HEADED MONSTER

I went through the drug recovery program and eventually regained the post office job. But the addictions crept up and seized me once again. For the second time, my boss fired me due to drug use on the job.

For 10 months I gave up, crawling deeper and deeper into the cave of addictions. Unable to sleep, sometimes for days, I laid on my bed at night, sweating and shaking. The more I craved cocaine, the more I used it. My tolerance increased to a point where I was using an ounce per week — a tremendous amount.

Anxiety, insomnia and headaches plagued me. Sometimes when I was drunk or high, I didn't recognize my own family. I stumbled home and fell into bed, only to spend the night in a cold sweat, my body trembling.

My children grew up before my eyes. We lived in the same house, but they were almost strangers to me. Because addictions consumed so much of my life, I had little time or energy left for them. And very little love. They saw that I valued my own needs above theirs, and they responded with avoidance.

"Hi," I greeted one of my sons as he arrived home from school. He was about 10 years old.

"Hi, Dad," he muttered, a scowl covering his face. He ducked into the bedroom he shared with his brothers and closed the door. I sensed that he disliked me — that he was ashamed of me. My heart felt heavy, yet empty. I knew something was missing. I craved love from my wife and kids. Yet what could I do? The drugs, the drinking — they had a hold on me too strong to break. They filled the cavity I felt deep in my soul. They made me feel happy and satisfied — if only for a moment.

I continued to hide in the dark cave of addiction until 1995. I again regained my post office job in 1994 and felt that I'd made some improvements. Then, in 1995, my wife and I began to experience problems in our marriage. Our oldest sons, now in high school, had gotten involved with drugs and gang violence. My wife's frustration turned toward me, and as we discussed the problem, I felt a surge of guilt. Two of my sons were doing drugs because of me. Instead of reaching out to them and to my wife, I got angry and pulled back.

"I can't stop!" I told her. "Don't ask me to stop." Again I felt the grip of my addictions, like a cold hand gripping my neck. I couldn't escape.

"José, the drugs are killing you. Please, it's not too late …"

"No!" I shook my head. "I have to handle this myself. I'm going away for a while." I grabbed a small suitcase and packed several clothing items. She left the room, knowing that she could not change my mind. I left our house that evening and went to stay with my mother.

A few days later, I called Pastor Robert at the First Assembly of God in Paramount, where we sent the kids to church. I asked if he could meet with me because I needed some help. Finally, I was ready to reach out to someone else.

Pastor Robert welcomed me into his office the next day.

## SLAYING THE THREE-HEADED MONSTER

"José, I'm glad to see you," he said with a smile. "What do you need to talk about?"

He already knew about my drug addiction, but I told him again. Then I told him about my marriage problems. When I reached the heart of the issue, I felt almost sick to my stomach.

"And now my older sons are getting involved in the street scene," I said. "They've joined gangs, and they're doing drugs. I don't want them to end up like … me." I swallowed, leaning over the desk, feeling ashamed.

Pastor Robert opened one of his desk drawers and pulled something out. A book. He set it on the wooden desktop and pushed it gently toward me.

I looked at it. *Holy Bible*, the front cover proclaimed in gold-embossed lettering.

"I want you to have this, José," said Pastor Robert. "This book can help you much more than I can. I recommend that you start reading here." He flipped the crisp pages and let the book fall open to the section he wanted. "The book of John."

Finally, I felt desperate enough to try anything. "Okay," I said. "I'll read it."

"Good. And come to church on Sundays." He paused and looked me in the eye. "Your problems feel too big for you to handle, and they are. But God can handle them, José. You just have to let him."

I read the book of John and felt impressed by the kindness of Jesus. Something about him had always attracted me, but I didn't see how the old stories I grew up hearing in Catholic school had any relevance to my life. But now, as I read the Bible myself and heard Pastor Robert speak on Sundays, I started to believe there was something to the stories. Perhaps Jesus wanted to help me.

☙☙☙

Over the next few years, my wife and I regularly attended church. I moved back in with her, and we tried to deal with our kids' problems, but throughout this time I never stopped abusing drugs. Although I believed what I'd learned in church — that Jesus was real and he wanted to save me — I couldn't seem to carry out my good intentions from Sunday through the rest of the week. I was stuck in the cave of addiction with the three-headed monster guarding the exit.

In 2000, I decided to make a public commitment to God. Pastor Robert baptized me, dunking me under water in front of my family and all the other church members. My baptism was a happy occasion, and I did celebrate — but in the days that followed, I recognized how far I still had to go. Drugs still ruled my life. I acted like a Christian on Sundays and wanted to believe that my life was changing, but I was living a lie. I would go to church and sing songs on Sunday, but on Monday I'd snort cocaine again.

For several years, I continued to live with only half my heart turned toward God. I believed that he had good plans for me, but I didn't know how to make them happen. Going to church felt like a façade. Although I wanted to change and I tried my hardest, the addictions remained too strong for me.

In 2002, we moved to Colton, but we still drove to Paramount for church. Eventually, however, we slacked off because of rising gas prices.

In April 2006, I was driving by Colton First Assembly of God and saw a number of cars in the parking lot. Hardly knowing why, I pulled into the paved lot and got out of my car.

Inside the building, I heard music. An usher welcomed me to the auditorium, where an Easter play was in progress.

I took a seat and watched the story unfold. I remembered reading the book of John several years previously, and I held my breath as that story came to life before my eyes.

"Crucify him! Crucify him!" jeered the crowd of white-robed people around Jesus as the climax of the story approached. The actor who portrayed Jesus looked out at the auditorium and cast his eyes downward. They seized him and dragged him away. Then they lifted him to a cross and nailed him to the boards. Jesus cried out with intense agony.

"Father, forgive them," he said, "for they know not what they do."

Deep in my heart, a ray of light illuminated the truth I had never really believed. Jesus died for me. He died to set me free from the bad decisions, from the drugs, from the selfishness that dragged me down and kept me from sharing love with my family. Suddenly, a clear picture of my selfishness rose before my eyes. For years, I had consistently put my needs and desires before anyone else's. I had chosen to love myself instead of God or my family.

I had slacked off on attending my old church, so it made sense to begin attending the Colton church after I saw the Easter play. The following year, my wife pulled me aside when I got home from working at the post office.

"I need to tell you something," she said. We went into our bedroom and shut the door.

"What is it?" I asked. Her tone and look told me it was something bad.

"It's our son," she said. "He's been arrested." She choked on the words.

I held her to my chest as she wept, and I thought about what to do. Guilt swept over me like a tidal wave. My stepson had made poor decisions, and now he was incarcerated. Instead of feeling frustrated with him, though, I felt angry with myself.

"How can I expect my son to be better when he has never had a father?" I asked bitterly.

She shook her head and hugged me, but I knew that I was right. My children grew up without a relationship with their father, and it was my fault. Instead of investing in them, I had invested in my addictions. The ray of light that had dawned in my heart during the Easter play reappeared, growing stronger and stronger.

## SLAYING THE THREE-HEADED MONSTER

I began to pray for my sons, but the guilt I felt still held me in its grasp. In the summer of 2008, I traveled to Boston with some friends and, out of my usual context, gave in to temptation. All week, I snorted cocaine and drank heavily. When I arrived back in California, I felt disgusted with myself. Suddenly, I knew what I needed to do — and for the first time, I was desperate enough to do it.

I fell to my knees and began to pray. I asked God to forgive me for all the ways I had ignored and defied his help through the many years of my life. I told him I had cheated myself out of a relationship with my children and asked him to forgive me.

"Please, Jesus," I prayed with head bowed and knees on the floor, "put the love in my heart that was never there. Fix the relationships that are lost. Give me another chance. I need your help, because I can't do anything without you."

I made a commitment to God that I would pray for my sons every day. I promised him that I would be faithful, that I would do my part. Now I see that he has been faithful throughout my life, even during the long years when I ran away from his love.

The difficulties didn't end. Soon after, four of my sons were arrested on various charges. It was difficult at first, especially for my wife. When someone asked her how her sons were doing, she broke down and cried. Not all the pain was erased, and not all the mistakes were reversed.

But something changed after I made that promise to

## DEFYING CIRCUMSTANCE

God — after I gave him my entire life. Finally, I could believe that I am somebody and that I have a life worth living without the masks of drugs and alcohol. Jesus gave me the strength to stop drinking and taking drugs. I didn't have that strength inside myself. I know it came from him. Jesus loosened the grip of addiction.

After enabling me to stop abusing my body, God gave me a second chance at parenting. When one of my sons was arrested, his wife panicked. Overwhelmed with raising their young sons by herself, she fled their home and began to take crystal methamphetamine.

My four grandsons needed a place to live. Happy to have a stable home to offer, my wife and I adopted them. My grandchildren know a different man from the one their parents avoided. I am glad they will not remember me as a drug addict, but only as a loving grandparent.

My daughter recently struggled with drug addiction.

"I'm sorry for not being around when you were a little girl," I told her.

She took a breath. "I hated you then, Dad. But now I look at you and see that God has done a wonderful work in your life. You are the glue that keeps our family together now. It gives me courage. Maybe God can make me just as strong."

Every day, I pray for my children and their families. Several times a week, I join a group to pray at the church building. We tell each other about our troubles and talk to God together. It is a beautiful time, and I need the regular rhythm of talking to people about God and talking to God.

## SLAYING THE THREE-HEADED MONSTER

One morning a few years ago, I got out of bed very early to kneel on the floor and pray. I asked God to help my children, and I thanked him for changing my life. As I remembered the years of drug dealing, of smoking marijuana, of drinking too much and snorting cocaine, I began to cry.

"Thank you, Jesus!" I said aloud. "Thank you for these memories — that they *are* memories and no longer realities. Thank you for saving me and giving me another chance to live. I could easily have died from an overdose, and I know my life is a gift."

I felt a tap on my shoulder. Opening my eyes, I saw my little grandson standing over me.

"Grandpa, you're crying," he said. His dark eyes were wide, concerned. "Please stop praying. I don't want you to be sad!"

I shook my head, smiling widely, and reached to hold him close to my chest. "No, it's all right. These are tears of joy! I am happy because God is so good."

The three-headed monster is dead. And I am alive.

# LIFE ON THE EDGE
## THE STORY OF JAMES
### WRITTEN BY KAREN KOCZWARA

"I'll shoot you right now!" The person in the ski mask waved the pistol like a mad man in the liquor store.

Hot rage took over my being. My life was falling apart, and this gunman was going to be sorry he messed with me.

"I lost my wife, I lost my kids, so you really think I care if I lose my life?!" I shouted back, slowly inching closer to him. I planned to snatch the gun right out of his hand.

Just as I was about to make my move, the second thief jumped over the counter from where he'd held the cashier at gunpoint. Both masked robbers fled.

I didn't stick around, either. Frantic thoughts consumed me as I walked to my cousin's house. Laura's face flashed into my mind; my beautiful wife, the one I'd hurt the most. How had I gotten here, a desperate man at the end of his rope? I knew death all too well — my best friend, my father, my baby son, all snatched from me before their time. And now I was losing Laura and my kids, too. I didn't care if I died. I was tired of running, tired of fighting.

☙☙☙

# DEFYING CIRCUMSTANCE

I was born on September 11, 1961. My family lived in a lower-class neighborhood in San Bernardino, California, where drugs were rampant. My petite, quiet mother raised my five sisters, three brothers and me with dignity. My father was mechanically inclined and worked at various shops. Though I watched my father drink daily as if he needed it to soften the rough edges of life, we were very close, and he taught me the value of hard work.

When I was 7, we moved into a safer neighborhood. My parents took us to church occasionally, but I wasn't impressed with it. I enjoyed the typical boy stuff: the outdoors, my friends and sports. But just before I entered junior high, I discovered something else I enjoyed more: marijuana.

"You ever smoked before, dude?" my friend asked one hot summer day.

I shook my head. "Nope."

"First time for everything." He lit a joint and handed it to me. I took a hit and immediately loved the way it made me feel. Suddenly, nothing seemed to matter. All my problems floated away as my head grew light. From that moment on, I was hooked.

Next, my older brother introduced me to inhalants. "This stuff gives you a whole new kind of high," he explained. He snagged some gas and spray paint from a local drug dealer, and we spent the afternoon getting high with my friend Curt. Again, I loved the euphoric feeling. I figured we weren't doing "real" drugs, so what was the harm?

## LIFE ON THE EDGE

When I was 14, my older sister and her husband went away for the weekend and left my brother and me the keys to her house. My brother broke into the liquor cabinet one night. "Check it out! They got all kinds of booze in here," he said excitedly, popping the cork off a bottle of wine.

"I dunno, man. What if they notice it's gone?" I hesitated.

"Nah, they won't. Look at all this." He gestured at the stash of bottles. "Whatcha gonna drink tonight, brother?"

I reluctantly selected a bottle of wine, and my brother opened a bottle of vodka. "This stuff's nasty straight," he groaned. "I'm gonna go to the liquor store and pick up some orange juice to make Screwdrivers. I'll take their truck."

A few minutes later, my brother raced back into the house, sweaty and panicked. "We gotta get out of here, man! I just wrecked their truck!"

"What are you talking about?" I demanded. My head was fuzzy from the alcohol, and I felt woozy as he rambled on. "How did you wreck his truck?"

"I dunno. I hit three cars. Put that stuff down, and let's get outta here!"

My father discovered what we'd done and disciplined us. "This had better be the last of your screwing around," he said sternly. "You're lucky no one got hurt tonight."

When high school rolled around, I busied myself with classes, played football and worked at a mechanic shop on the weekends. My father constantly impressed on me the importance of hard work. But as a 15-year-old boy, I had only two things on my mind: girls and partying.

I continued smoking pot and drinking and soon discovered more serious drugs like acid, crank and speed. I didn't care which drug I took; I only cared about getting high. I casually dated girls and managed to keep up my grades and my job, but I lived for the weekends when I could get wasted with my friends.

One weekend, my friends Curt and Mark invited me to an all-night party at some new friends' house. "They're older, and they can get their hands on booze," they told me. "You in?"

A few hours into the party, Curt and I decided to grab something to eat. I borrowed our friend's 1969 4-speed Firebird, figuring he wouldn't notice if I was gone for a bit. I slid behind the wheel, Curt jumped into the passenger seat and we sped down the road. "Let's see what this thing can really do," I said, excitement mounting as the speedometer crept higher and higher. I pressed the gas to the floor, and we climbed the steep hill, soon reaching 80 miles per hour.

"Whew! Awesome!" I hollered.

As I veered into a turn, the car spun completely around and ran smack into a telephone pole. I slammed on the brakes, and the gas gauge popped up and hit me in the face. I flew back against the seat, my heart racing as the car came to a screeching halt. "Sh**," I muttered. "You okay, Curt?"

"Dude, you better wipe down your fingerprints and get out of here," he said, yanking open the passenger door.

# LIFE ON THE EDGE

"Those guys are gonna kill us when they see this car." He ran down the street, leaving me alone with the damage.

When I finally stopped shaking, I drove the dented car back to our friend's house, parked it in the driveway and sauntered back into the party as though nothing had happened. To my relief, everyone was wasted. A fight had broken out in the back room, so no one noticed.

Soon, getting wasted on the weekends wasn't enough, and my friends and I looked for ways to get drunk at school. I had a body shop class every morning, and though I enjoyed working with my hands, I always sought to spice things up. My friend Jake snuck a bottle of Red Velvet into class one day, and we chugged it until it was gone.

"Dude, there you go again, back into the Jake Trance," I teased as he stumbled like a zombie. "We gotta get you outta here. Let me just grab something from the cafeteria first."

As I stood in line for my food, two notoriously loud-mouthed guys threw racial comments my way. "Who you talkin' to?" I demanded. On impulse, I dove at them, and we fought, throwing punches and chasing each other around the room. At last, the principal hauled us off, and I was expelled.

"Enough is enough around here, James," he said sternly as we sat face to face in his office. "You've been given plenty of chances, but this school won't tolerate your behavior anymore."

He sent me to a continuation school, where I finished out high school. I found work at a local diesel truck stop;

drug dealers down the street supplied everything from speed to coke to pot. I soon learned the ropes and started selling drugs myself. Within no time, I was making far more than minimum wage. I bought myself a motorcycle, a used car and some fancy new clothes. Though I tried to fly under the radar, my father eventually grew suspicious of my new purchases. I grew tired of his rules, and after graduation I moved in with my cousin in Albuquerque.

I lived there for three months and continued using drugs. Days blurred together as I experienced one bad acid trip after another. My father came out to visit one week. We went for a long walk, and he begged me to come home. "Your mom's worried about you," he said with a sigh. "You need to get your act together, James, become a real man. I think you should join the Navy. It will be good discipline."

I stared at him. "The Navy?" I'd never considered joining the military. I hadn't considered my future much at all, actually. Deep down, I knew I couldn't continue this way forever, hopping from house to house, doing drugs and getting into trouble. Perhaps a drastic change might be just the right thing.

I returned home and joined the Navy a week later. "You're making a good choice, son," my father encouraged me. I hoped he was right.

I went to Camp Nimitz for boot camp and enlisted in the drill division. From there, I went on to school in Illinois, all the while continuing to smoke pot and drink. I returned to San Diego, where I worked at sea repairing

## LIFE ON THE EDGE

ships for two years. During this time, I got orders to re-enlist. My contract guaranteed me a job in the advanced air conditioning repair field — a lucrative career. But I was young and homesick and wanted out of the nomadic life of the military.

☙☙☙

One fall evening, I went to my cousin's house for a birthday party. We stayed up late, drinking, doing drugs and making noise until the cops broke up the party. I was so wasted, I could hardly keep my eyes open, but a friend and I got in the car, anyway. Not far down the road, I completely fell asleep at the wheel.

Weeks passed as I lay in a coma, fighting for my life, my mother and grandmother weeping over me in prayer.

When I finally regained consciousness, my dad was there.

"There's a cop outside the door waiting to arrest you," he said. "They're charging you with manslaughter."

My friend was dead.

The judge found me guilty. I was devastated. I had killed my friend, and now I would have to serve time in prison for what I had done. My night of partying had cost both of us our lives.

I was sentenced to prison in Susanville, California, but due to overpopulation in the system, I was taken to one of the harshest prisons in America: San Quentin. I heard horrid things about this place which housed California's only gas chamber and death row and was home to some of the state's most notorious criminals. But nothing could have prepared me for the hell I encountered upon walking through those doors.

A cacophony of yelling and cursing echoed through the dismal halls as a guard escorted me to my cell. I tried to shut out the noise as he slammed the barred door, leaving me alone in a stifling cubicle of a room. A sliver of sunlight poked through the window above as I slumped onto the bottom metal bunk. I stared at the sleeves of my orange jumpsuit as the yelling escalated; everyone was angry with someone, it seemed — themselves, the world, the guy next to them. *I'm not like these guys,* I thought to myself. *I didn't kill anyone on purpose. I don't belong here.*

My cellmate gave me the rundown on the place I'd call home for the next 14 weeks. "Look, man, this place is crazy. You don't want to mess with nobody. Don't disrespect anyone, and don't let them disrespect you. And don't borrow anything from anyone, you hear? That's just askin' for trouble. Just keep to yourself, and you'll be okay."

It was December, and the cold marine air crept in, chilling me to the bone. Someone gave me a beanie; beanies were like gold in prison, as our thin jumpsuits did little to warm us up. One afternoon, a fellow inmate snatched it off my head.

"Hey, man! What the h*** do you think you're doing?" I cried as the guy ran off.

## LIFE ON THE EDGE

A guard stood nearby, watching me closely. I jumped up and approached him. "Look, man, I gotta take care of this guy. He can't go disrespectin' me like that."

The guard raised an eyebrow. "Do what you have to do," he said with a shrug.

I crept up on the inmate and kicked him hard from behind with my boot. He whirled around and shoved me back against the concrete. "You wanna mess with me?" He lunged at me. I fought back, kicking him repeatedly in the face, the gut and anywhere else I could reach. We pounded on each other, blood spurting on the ground as we went round and round. The guard stood by and watched, and to my surprise, no one broke us up. I gave the guy one final kick and walked away in disgust.

I was released from San Quentin shortly after and sent to Susanville, then back to Chino Prison to complete my sentence. In just a short time, the prison system had hardened me. I knew how to deal with the guys on the streets, but dealing with violent, stir-crazy criminals was a different game. To keep from going insane, I spent my time at the prison gym lifting weights. A scrawny, cheerful guy named Sam often lifted weights beside me. One day, he approached me with a question.

"Hey, James. I see what you do every day. Why don't you come see what I do now?" he asked.

I set down my barbell. "What you talkin' about, Sam?"

"I go to this Bible study here. You wanna come with me sometime?"

"A Bible study? I dunno, Sam."

## DEFYING CIRCUMSTANCE

"You'll like it. Tomorrow morning? What do you say?"

I smiled. I liked Sam, and it seemed he liked me, too. "All right, man. I'll be there." As he walked away, I chuckled to myself. *A Bible study. What have I gotten myself into?*

To my surprise, I liked the Bible study more than I thought I would. The leader shared about God's love, explaining that no matter what we'd done in our past, we could find forgiveness for our wrongdoings if we simply asked. "We're all here because we've messed up," the leader began. "We broke the law, and this is our consequence. We've also broken God's laws, and the consequence for that is the death penalty. But we can be pardoned! Jesus loves us so much that he stood in for us when he was executed on a cross. We get a fresh start if we just ask him to forgive us for messing up. Just accept God's love, and ask him to help you know him more each day."

"That's pretty good stuff," I told Sam that afternoon. "Maybe you can tell me a little bit more about this God in the Bible."

"Sure," Sam said. He shared how God had turned his life around and how he had chosen to forgive himself and believe that God had forgiven him for his past, too. "I'm really excited about where I'm at, because I have hope for the first time in my life," he said with a smile. "You can have hope, too, James."

The more I talked with Sam, the more I wanted this relationship with God. That May, I asked God to give me a clean slate and replace the hurt and guilt in my heart with hope and peace. It had taken me 25 years to realize that God loved me, and now I wanted to know him more than anything else. I was still a prisoner behind bars, but because of God, I had been set free!

I spent that summer reading my Bible, praying and learning all I could about God. Sam remained an encouragement, accompanying me to Bible studies inside the prison.

I was released in August and went to live with my sister in Riverside. I got a job as a driver for a concrete company and tried to focus on getting back on my feet. I reported for work at 4 a.m. and often worked until the sun went down, leaving little time for church or friends. As life got busy, I slid back into my old ways and put God aside.

My father passed away the following year on Christmas Day, and I was devastated by the loss. No one that close to me had died before, and it hit me hard. Though I'd given my father a bad time over the years, he was a good role model, reminding me to work hard and stay on the right path. I was sad we didn't have more time together, and to cope with my pain, I returned to partying.

One afternoon, while driving down the road, I saw a sign for a car wash fundraiser. I pulled into the parking lot and chatted with an attractive woman outside. "You gonna get your car washed or what?" she asked with a smile after we flirted for a while.

I laughed. "Oh, yeah, sure. But only if I can get your phone number."

## DEFYING CIRCUMSTANCE

"My name's Laura," she said, blushing as she wrote down her number.

Laura and I began hanging out, and I enjoyed her company. Not only was she beautiful, but she was calm, smart, funny and sweet, too. Laura loved God and encouraged me to get back into church. "I know, I need to go," I said with a sigh. "I'm just so darn busy these days."

We married about a year later and not long after, had a beautiful little girl. I worked hard to provide for my new family, but on the side, I continued drinking, using drugs and partying. *I'm not hurting anyone,* I figured. *I'm being faithful to Laura, taking care of the family and bringing in the dough.* Deep down, though, I knew the truth. I had chosen to numb the pain from my father's loss with drugs and work instead of seeking comfort from the God I met in prison. In 1989, our first son was born. We were thrilled to have both a girl and a boy in the house! One night, when he was just a few weeks old, I put him to bed around 11 p.m. and went back in the living room to watch the Lakers' basketball game. At 1 a.m., I went back in to check on him and, to my horror, discovered he wasn't breathing. Panicked, I scooped him out of his crib; he was pale and limp in my arms. "Baby's not breathing!" I cried frantically.

We sped down the road to the nearest hospital. I jumped out of the car and raced into the emergency room with my tiny son in my arms. "My baby's not breathing! Help, someone help!" I cried.

A nurse snatched him from my arms and hurried to

the back while I stood there, praying that my son would not die. I paced the floor for what felt like hours until a doctor emerged with a solemn look on his face. "I'm sorry, but there was nothing we could do. Your son is dead."

*Dead.* I went numb. First my father, and now my son? How could this be happening? I sank into a vinyl chair and sobbed for the little boy I would never hold again. I'd thought I had it all: a beautiful wife, two kids and a decent job. Now, in a devastating blow, I'd lost what was most precious to me.

I resorted to selling drugs. One night, while I was high, I cheated on my wife. I was angry with myself for losing control, but even more angry at life for beating me up. I held onto my job and managed to function at work and home, while being constantly high. My wife's eyes grew sad as I became more distant. "Look, what do you want? I'm puttin' food on the table, okay?" I reminded her. But she only wanted what every woman does: She wanted my heart.

One night, while driving home from a party, I heard the dreaded sound of sirens behind me. I panicked, as a sawed-off shotgun sat on the console next to the driver's seat. If they caught me with it, I'd be toast. Instead of slowing, I impulsively stepped on the gas and veered around the corner. The cops followed me, and our game of cat and mouse soon became a high-speed chase. I pulled up to a friend's driveway, tossed the shotgun and ran for the house. But it was too late. The cops had seen the gun, and they arrested me.

## DEFYING CIRCUMSTANCE

"Looks like you already got a record, huh?" the cop said as he shoved me in the back of his patrol car. "Do you know the penalty for evading the police while carrying a deadly weapon?"

"Yes, sir," I mumbled. How could I have been so careless?

I was sent to prison for a second time, leaving my devastated wife behind with our daughter at home. When I got out, my wife announced she was pregnant again. I tried to make up for lost time by being as nurturing as possible. I attended Lamaze class with her, rubbed her feet and told her I loved her. But on the side, I kept up my double life and returned to selling drugs. I was so far into my reckless lifestyle at this point I could not see my way out.

Just a few days after Christmas, I sold a friend some drugs. He told me he couldn't pay right away. "It's cool. Just pay me when you can," I told him.

But two weeks later, when he still hadn't paid up, I grew angry. "I knew I shouldn't have sold to that kid," I muttered.

"Let's go talk to him," my brother suggested. "We'll be cool, calm, just tell him we want our money."

"Fine," I relented.

When my friend opened the door, I tried to explain we had come in peace. "I just want my money," I said calmly. If he was smart, he'd pay up, and we could simply go on our way.

My friend's eyes grew angry. Another guy appeared

# LIFE ON THE EDGE

behind him, and before I knew what was happening, they attacked me, jumping on me and trying to stab me with a knife. Suddenly, a third guy jumped out with a shotgun, and I dove for it before he could shoot. We tussled on the floor of the living room for a few minutes. He slammed me against the wall so hard it knocked the wind out of me, and I struggled to get back up. The second guy broke a leg off the wooden dinette table and swung at me. I ducked. He missed. He swung again, hitting me on the back, then the head. As I tried to regain my strength, I heard a *click*. The first guy had fired the gun at me, but it hadn't gone off.

Adrenaline surged through my veins as I struggled to stand up and stumble toward the front door. "Just let it go, all right, guys? We didn't mean no harm," I mumbled as I walked away. Shaken, I staggered down the road, unable to believe I'd nearly been killed in what should have been a peaceful confrontation. I'd have to stop messing with the wrong people and be more careful next time.

Though my friends went back and encouraged the guys not to press charges, they did, anyway, and I received a violation on my parole. I was sent back to prison for a third time.

Just a week after I arrived at Chino Prison, our third child, Martin, arrived. I felt terrible I was not present for his birth, especially since I'd attended Lamaze classes in preparation for the big day. My wife called a few days after he was born to deliver bad news. "Martin has spinal meningitis. They think he caught some infection in the hospital. It can be life threatening, especially in babies his size, so he's being transferred to University Hospital. It's one of the best in the nation, so he'll be in good hands." She tried to stay strong as she shared the devastating diagnosis.

"Oh, man." I hung up the phone and prayed. I hadn't talked to God much since I got out of prison the first time, and I hoped he still heard my prayers. "Please, God, let my son be okay. We can't lose another child. We just can't."

My wife stayed by our son's side as the doctors pumped antibiotics into his tiny body. She called one night with an extraordinary story. "I was at my end today, so scared and sad. I went to the chapel and prayed by the candlelight, begging God to heal our baby. While I was praying, I felt someone tap me on the shoulder and say, 'Don't worry. Your son is going to be okay.' When I looked behind me, no one was there. I went back up to the room, and the doctors announced Martin was taking a turn for the better. James, he's going to be okay!"

I was stunned and elated. "Oh, man, thank God," I whispered. God had heard our prayers. Our son was going to be okay! "So, who tapped you on the shoulder?" I asked slowly.

"Maybe it was an angel," she said quietly.

Sam said angels were real, that God sometimes sent them to comfort and protect people. Was it possible one visited my wife at her hour of desperation? Either way, God answered our prayers. I wished I could be there to see my son and hug my wife.

## LIFE ON THE EDGE

☙☙☙

My son was 7 months old when I got out of prison and met him for the first time. "Wow, he's so beautiful," I murmured, admiring his big blue eyes and perfect features. I squeezed his tiny fingers. "Daddy's sorry he wasn't here for you, little fella, but he's here now," I said.

Our fourth child, a daughter, was born next. With our growing family, I knew I had to step up and stay out of trouble, but somehow, I always found my way back to drugs. I held various jobs to put food on the table, but tension grew in our home. Laura was weary of my destructive ways and wanted stability for our family. "You're here, but you're not present, James," she told me wearily. "How can I trust you not to get in trouble again? You're walkin' on thin ice with the law. How many more times you gonna put us through this?"

"I'm gonna change," I assured her, but even as I said the words, I wondered if I really could. I'd been smoking pot since I was 13 and couldn't imagine a life without drugs or booze. Since I'd always been able to function and work, I didn't consider myself as bad as the guys on the streets. In the back of my mind, I knew I needed to turn back to God for help, but I wasn't sure he'd want much to do with me after all I'd done.

On Father's Day, I piled the kids into the car, and we drove to my mother's house to celebrate. I'd had a few too many beers at our celebration when I buckled the kids in the car and headed home. A car darted out in front of our vehicle, and we crashed. "Everyone okay? Kids?" I cried frantically, scrambling to get to the backseat.

"My door's stuck! I can't get out!" my daughter cried. At last, she climbed across my seat and pried open the driver's side door. We all climbed out, shaken and bruised, but alive. When the cops arrived on the scene, the children were their first concern.

"Everyone okay here? Need an ambulance?" a cop asked, rushing to our side.

I shook my head. "I think we're okay." My legs shook as I juggled the baby in my arms. To my relief, she let out a healthy, strong cry.

We soon learned the other driver had been drinking as well. As I tucked my kids into bed that night, I gave them extra hugs and kisses, thanking God for protecting us all from what could have been a devastating or even deadly accident.

In 1996, my next son came along. Our house was now bursting at the seams, and Laura was more tired than ever. She put up a good front, caring for the kids, cooking dinner and doing the laundry, but the vacant look in her eyes was now permanent. We fought often, sometimes about money, sometimes about the kids, but mostly about my bad habits. One day, we got into an especially heated fight on the front porch.

"Look, what do you want from me? You're always on my back, nagging me about my stuff! I'm goin' to church with you, even helpin' around that place on the weekends, and I'm providing for the family. Why don't you just back off?" I yelled. We continued fighting until the cops showed up.

"Heard there's fighting going on over here," the cop said when he got out of his car.

"No, we're fine," I lied, glaring at my wife.

"If I have to come back again, you're going with me," the cop warned before he drove off.

But one night, not long after that fight, I grew especially angry and punched my wife. As she stumbled backward, I realized I'd gone too far this time.

She called the cops, and they hauled me back to jail for six months. While in jail, I thought long and hard about my life. Though I had been attending church regularly with my wife, I did it mostly to keep her off my back. God had become my go-to guy in time of crisis but nothing more.

When I got out of jail, I returned to drinking and drugs. One evening, my buddy came over to have a few beers. As we sat on the front porch, my wife came out and yelled at me. "You know what, James? I'm done! I can't do this anymore. I've put up with your crap for years, but this is enough. You get out of jail and go right back to your stuff the very next day. I'm done." She stormed back into the house.

I was already in hot water with the cops; if she called them again, I'd be hauled right back to prison. Panicked, I ran into the house, grabbed a huge plastic water bottle full of coins and ran down to my cousin's house a quarter of a mile away. I stashed the coins at his house, grabbed a few from the bottle and headed to the liquor store, where I bought a 24-ounce Budweiser and a giant Snickers bar.

"What brings you in here this late?" my friend Mark asked from behind the counter.

"Just trouble with the woman at home," I mumbled, counting out my coins.

Suddenly, a guy in a ski mask came from behind me, jumped over the counter and yelled at Mark, "Give me all your money!"

"Okay, okay," Mark said, hands shaking as he opened the register.

"Not that money. I know you got more in back," the guy barked.

As I turned around, a second masked thief waved a pistol like a mad man. "I'll shoot you right now!" he threatened.

Hot rage took over my being. My life was falling apart, and this gunman was going to be sorry he messed with me.

"I lost my wife, I lost my kids, so you really think I care if I lose my life?!" I shouted back, slowly inching closer to him. I planned to snatch the gun right out of his hand.

Just as I was about to make my move, the second thief jumped over the counter from where he'd held the cashier at gunpoint. Both masked robbers fled.

Shaken, that night I couldn't stop thinking about how my life had come to this. Something had to change if I had any hope of saving my family. Something had to change for my life to be worth living. And that something was me.

# LIFE ON THE EDGE

The next day, after work, I showed up at my kids' basketball practice. I was sober for once, and when I saw my wife in the bleachers, I approached her. "Look, I know you're angry with me, but can we talk?" I asked.

She glared at me. "James, I'm tired, okay? Just leave me alone. Get out of here."

As the kids laughed and cheered in the background, their shoes squeaking against the basketball court, I slowly turned to leave. Despondent, I drove down the road in a daze. What if Laura really meant it? What if she was really done with me? Could I hardly blame her after all I'd put her through?

As I turned down the corner, the church I attended sometimes with my wife, Colton First Assembly of God, came into view. On impulse, I pulled into the parking lot. A service was in progress, and I slid into a seat in the back as the pastor spoke. After the service, a guy tapped me on the shoulder.

"James, you okay?" he asked.

He looked me straight in the eye. "James, are you okay?" he asked again.

I took a deep breath. "I'm fine."

"You know what you need, man? You need discipline. Have you ever heard of a men's home?"

I shook my head. "No, what's that?"

"It's a place men go to get the discipline and direction they need. Some men are sent there by the courts, and others turn themselves in. What do you think?"

I took another deep breath. *Discipline.* My father had

driven that word into my head many times. Could that really be the secret to a better life? "I'm willing to give it a try," I said slowly. "What do I have to do?"

"I'll give you the number to call. Call every day until you get in."

I went back to my cousin's house and thought about what the guy had said. I was at the end of my rope. Laura wanted nothing to do with me, I was on the verge of losing my kids and I'd spent the last few years in and out of prison. Did I really want to keep living this way? I picked up the phone and called the men's home. I called daily, and a week later, I got in.

"Come on down tomorrow morning," the guy on the other end said.

As I packed my things, I grew excited. This could be the beginning of my new life.

I arrived at the men's home at 8 a.m. the next morning. An intake counselor sat me down for a brief interview about what I'd been through. "James, here's the deal," he explained. "Your wife has been through a lot. Between the cheating, the abuse, the violence and the drugs, she's really beat down. She's built a wall around her heart. God will crush that wall, but it's not going to happen overnight. Now, we have a Bible study that meets in an hour, and you're more than welcome to come. Or you can go up to your room and spend some time by yourself. But at 6 a.m. tomorrow morning, you're the men's home property, and you'll do what we ask you to do."

I processed his words, not sure what to make of

everything. "I'm gonna go upstairs for now. See you tomorrow morning," I said, standing. "Thanks for having me here."

I went upstairs to my room and sat on my bed. *Your wife has built a wall around her heart.* The words echoed in my mind over and over. It made sense; I knew I'd hurt Laura deeply. But was coming here really the answer? Suddenly, other thoughts took over my mind: *What are you doing here, James? You're a decent guy. You provide for your family, you show up for your kids. You're being a little tough on yourself, don't you think?* Then, just as quickly as those thoughts entered my mind, another set of thoughts shouted louder: *James, you take care of business here. You don't belong at home right now; you belong here.*

All day, the thoughts went back and forth in my mind like a battle. At last, I picked up a Bible and flipped it open. My eyes fell onto a passage in Matthew 6:33: "Seek first the kingdom of God and his righteousness and all these things will be added unto you." I read it over, the words sinking in. *Seek first HIS kingdom.* As the words penetrated my heart, I crumpled to the floor and wept.

Though I had met God in prison, I had never tried to do things his way or build a real relationship with him. I'd carried him around like a good luck charm in my back pocket, but he wasn't important to my everyday life. When things got tough, I'd turned to drugs, violence and abuse to ease the pain, but none worked. Instead, my life became more destructive and meaningless. Now, alone in this room, I realized just how simple it was. I needed one thing and one thing only: I needed Jesus.

"God, thank you," I prayed through my tears. "Thank you for never letting me go, even when I turned away from you. Forgive me for the wrong I've done. I now know you're all I need. I want to seek first your kingdom. Please, God, use me. I want to spend the rest of my life with a purpose."

Any remnants of my skepticism about the men's home disappeared that night. I awoke ready to serve my time and learn how to change. The days were regimented from the moment we got up to the moment we went to bed, much like the military. I wished I had heeded my father's words at the time and stayed in the Navy, but I'd been young and naive and thought I could take on the world by myself. Now, I had an opportunity to step up and be a real man. God had given me a second chance.

I worked hard at the men's home, attending Bible studies and performing my duties around the place. I was soon respected and asked to be one of the drivers for the home. My mother and sister visited often and brought my kids with them. My eyes lit up as my little ones scampered into my arms. "Oh, Daddy misses you so much!" I cried. "I need to stay here a little bit longer, but I'll be home soon, I promise."

I didn't see my wife at all for the first four months. It was the longest 120 days of my life. I desperately missed her and wanted her to know I was a sincerely changed man. But on the other side of town, she hit her knees every night, praying that God would make me into the man he wanted me to be. When she finally visited, I gripped her tightly, but as she pulled away, I saw the skepticism in her eyes.

"I'm not the same man anymore, I promise," I told her, my eyes pleading. "God has done some amazing things in my heart since I've been here. He's really humbled me, and I no longer want anything to do with the things of my past. I'm a new man."

"I want to believe you, James. I really do. I've been praying so much for you, and I've missed you. I know you're in the right place," she said softly.

After six months, I left the men's home. My friend set me up with a job building movie sets. But I had started attending church more frequently and had gotten to know several of the leaders. "James, we've seen your work around here," they said. "You do a good job. How would you like to work for the church?"

"Really?" I was flattered and accepted their offer, which included more pay than the movie set job! I poured myself into my new work, overseeing landscaping and various projects around the church. I wished my father was still alive, as I knew he'd be proud of me. He'd always been a man of his hands and had taught me how to be one, too. More importantly, though, I wished he could see the changed person I'd become. *I'm a real man now, Dad.*

My kind, patient wife took me back into her arms and our home. Just as that counselor had promised, the walls around her heart slowly crumbled, and she was able to trust me again as I proved to her I'd changed. "I'm not sure I would have put up with me all that time," I told her one night. "You really are amazing."

"It was tough at times," she admitted. "I was tired of it all and ready to give up. But God helped me love you even when you hurt me the most. I prayed for you every day, and my prayers were answered. You've become the husband and father I always knew you could be."

I got involved with various other ministries around church, including the boys' program and the church choir. I played Judas in the church Easter production. As I sang my heart out, I thanked God that I'd found a new place to belong, a new group of friends who loved God and loved me for who I was.

The hardened man of my past was behind me, replaced by a husband and father who loved God and wanted to share that love with others.

≈≈≈

"Hey, James, can you pray for me?" a church member asked one day.

"Sure," I replied. "What's going on?"

As he shared his struggles, I nodded empathetically. "I was there once, too," I told him. "The Bible reads in Proverbs 3:5: 'Trust in the Lord with all your heart and lean not on your own understanding; in all your ways acknowledge him and he will make your paths straight.' I was a messed-up guy, thinking I could do it all on my

## LIFE ON THE EDGE

own, trying to lean on my own understanding. *He's* the only one who could make my paths straight."

As I drove home that night, I thanked God once again for bringing me to Colton First Assembly of God. But more importantly, I thanked him for saving my life. Not only had he pulled me from the brink of death several times, but he had given me a new life. I no longer lived on the edge, but my life was more exciting than ever. And there was no turning back.

# MASTER IN THE MESSAGE
## THE STORY OF ELENA
### WRITTEN BY RICHARD DREBERT

Excommunicated.

As a mother of four, I didn't *feel* like a heretic …

The funeral-faced Catholic bishop adjusted his dark robe. "Divorce is a curse, Elena. Marriage is a permanent sacrament. It endures until one of you dies."

"But *I'm* not getting the divorce. Juan is divorcing me!"

The bishop's office held a chill, like a basement full of meat. My little daughters, Julia and Daniella, played on a Persian rug near a teetering floor lamp, and I wrestled Marie and Jacob on my lap as Jesus stared down at me from his big golden cross on a wall.

The bishop looked grave as he said, "In our diocese we are very strict in these matters. I'm sorry."

I nodded resolutely and gathered up my four jewels. Walking slowly past pews and gilded pulpit, I studied the figures set in the stained-glass windows from *inside* the sanctuary for the last time. Frustration and shame convulsed from my heart in great teardrops as I drove home.

I spoke to my children who crawled over the crumpled divorce papers that Juan had served me: "Everybody who loves me is gone. And now I have lost my church, too?"

## DEFYING CIRCUMSTANCE

My next words I kept from my babies' ears, but I shouted them in my head: *If God has forsaken me, I shall live for the devil!*

❧❧❧

I was born in Trinidad, Colorado, east of the Sangre de Cristo (Blood of Christ) mountains. Mexican families had settled in the New Mexico Territory after the region was ceded to the United States following the Mexican-American War. Trinidad is about 20 miles north of the New Mexico/Colorado border.

I never learned my grandfather's native tongue when I was a girl, and some of Grandpa's Spanish ways died with him in a horrible accident in a coal mine. His family had joined work crews that kept the Trinidad mines thriving in the late 1800s. The coal beds lay in the Raton Basin along the original Santa Fe Trail, and ox-drawn wagons moved loads of coal to the railroad at Trinidad. Hispanic families built adobe homes around town, and Trinidad grew into a metropolis run by coal-mining companies owned by men like the Rockefellers.

My first memories are of Grandma's old home on Convent Street, an inviting two-story palace to me. When snowdrifts crowded the doors, a big black coal stove heated the living room. My little gray-haired grandmother baked bread in a coal-fired kitchen stove, and she smoothed our clothes with a heavy iron, shaped like a boat with a wooden handle on top. She heated the little boat on

## MASTER IN THE MESSAGE

the stove top, and I could barely lift it when she let me try.

Grandma gathered her brood in her warm nest, nurturing my uncles, aunts and cousins. Her sons hunted deer in the forests around Trinidad, and we ate sumptuous meals with venison as the main course. Grandma sternly warned her tribe of grandchildren against playing in the basement, but we peeked down the mysterious stairs when an adult opened the door. In my uncles' bloody sanctum, venison hung in thin strips upon clotheslines, drying into jerky. Slabs of meat cured above the cool earthen floor.

I loved walking with my cousins to a soda shop, the Trinidad Creamery, to lick ice cream cones or sip milkshakes. Everything about my home seemed stable in those days, until Mom and Dad loaded up our station wagon with all that we owned.

"California, here we come," Mom said, putting on a brave smile for my little sister, Judith, my two brothers and me. Mom's asthma troubled her more and more in the high Colorado altitude, and Dad knew he could get a job in Los Angeles with his craft. We honked goodbye as we left Grandma's house, looking forward to coming back to Trinidad to visit in the summers.

My hardworking father found a demand for his trade, making jewelry for stores and dentures for dentists. Mom enrolled me at a Catholic school called Saint Vibiana, adjacent to a cathedral that once entombed the 3rd-century Roman martyr. It seemed like the gates of heaven had opened to me when I sat in the great Cathedral of Los Angeles.

## DEFYING CIRCUMSTANCE

A tribute to Saint Vibiana summarized the demeanor that the nuns required of students:

*"Through your fasting and prayer you were given the grace to endure suffering and torment at the hands of your persecutors. Intercede for us, dear saint ..."*

I absorbed a satisfying piety at Vibiana, awestruck by the onyx and marble in her sanctuary, and desirous to imitate the kindness of the sisters. I joined the choir, though I had no idea what we were singing. The nuns taught us songs in Latin, and during Mass, the priests rambled in the language of the ancient Roman church.

Inside Vibiana, I sensed a peaceful presence that I attributed to God as I attended Mass, required by my parents. The nuns taught me to genuflect in "God's house" and obey the priest who represented God himself, a man who could absolve me from sins when I confessed to him.

But Mom's health slowly continued to go downhill. The Los Angeles smog clogged her lungs, and Dad moved us to San Bernardino, where the air was dryer and less full of particulates. Dad worked for dentists there, and when Mom gained back her strength, she landed a job with the San Bernardino County Hospital, cleaning and helping in the kitchen. Side by side, especially during my teens, Mom and I seemed more like sisters than mother and daughter — she had given birth to me when she was 15.

To anyone but a child, our move to the Highlands might have been a step down, and though our house was small, I loved our little farm. Dad brought home some big rowdy dogs that had acres to romp in. He built us cages to

# MASTER IN THE MESSAGE

raise rabbits and chickens. As the eldest daughter, Mom expected me to care for my brothers and sisters when she was at work, where she expended her waning energy. By the time I was 10, I could cook and clean like a grown woman.

I was in fourth grade when Mom enrolled me in my new Catholic school, Saint Ann, where my aptitude for sports showed up unexpectedly: I could really swish the net in basketball. And I was fast. I had great ball-handling skills and toured with our players to beat teams in other towns like Turner and Artesia. I excelled in the sport for the next four years and received a golden medal to mark my achievement as a basketball champion.

But the projects, called Waterman Gardens, changed my life. One day the buzzer on the basketball court sounded for the last time, signaling a new quarter in life when I attended public school. We moved away from our farm to the city, not far from church. I never missed Mass, but had to teach myself new skills to survive in a rough neighborhood.

"Just stay close," I told my sister and brothers as we approached the back of the big brick hardware store beyond the schoolyard. About 20 girls and boys milled around its windowless rear entrance near an overflowing trash bin. They smoked and talked, until they saw us and started moving in our direction. We crossed to the opposite street, but a dozen of them cut us off.

The Chicano girls started talking smack, and I strained

to understand them. I shook my head, knowing by their tone the words were insults.

"You can't even speak Spanish? You trying to be a *white* girl? You think you betta' than us?"

My Catholic-girl kindness wore out when one bully pulled Judith's hair and she began to cry a little. A girl shaped like a massive pear, with stringy black hair, shoved me, and I cut loose a slap that set the whole hoard on me like a bunch of angry hens. Somehow I herded my siblings down the street, fighting off punches and kicks, and finally home.

In junior high and high school, I swapped ball-handling practice for learning to street fight and could use my fists and feet as adeptly as I drove for a basket. Sometimes I could have avoided brawls, but somehow I enjoyed the challenge of besting a bully. After my ninth-grade year at San Bernardino High School, the bullies found easier marks, and I settled into a routine: cooking and cleaning at home, schoolwork and attending church religiously.

"Elena! Are you up?" Mom hollered.

Nancy, my best friend, blared her little car's horn at me in the driveway, and I rolled from beneath my covers. Forty days of Lent were almost over. I hadn't missed a single day attending morning services. I grabbed a coat, threw it on over my pajamas and slipped on my untied shoes. I rushed out the door with a hairbrush in my hand.

"We're going to be late, Elena! Were you still

sleeping?" Nancy drove like a maniac as I tried to brush snarls out of my dark hair.

Nancy and I vowed not to miss a day of morning Mass and communion on Lent each year. Duty to God consumed me, taking shape in a sterling record for attendance in church and school. If I made a commitment, I kept it. A laundry list of obligatory duties helped me maintain the Virgin Mary's divine favor.

My 10th grade couldn't have been better. I excelled in mathematics, and overall my grades were good. Juan fascinated me — a tall, proud Hispanic boy, who kept my father's strict rules so he could see me. He came from a good Mexican family and worked hard after school.

"He's here, Elena!" My little sister was as excited at seeing Juan as I was.

Mom liked him, too, but it irritated me that she refused to endorse him as "marriage material" for reasons she never put into words. In the three years before our wedding, all she would say was, "Juan's a nice boy, but he'll never be a good husband, Elena."

My graduation scored higher in my young life than any basketball tournaments I had ever won. Seeing me in my cap and gown crowned a moment of achievement for my mother and father, who believed their daughter had a bright future. But for me, graduation was a marker nearer my ultimate goal: marrying Juan. My temper flared if anyone criticized my objective, and my betrothed and I set a date for a June wedding.

My parents decided to be supportive, and I picked out

a wedding dress. My size three was still too baggy, and both sides had to be taken in! I picked my 12 bridesmaids, and my girlfriends decorated Our Lady of Guadalupe for a traditional Mexican wedding. My own Catholic priest performed the vows, and brilliant red roses adorned the reception hall. A Mexican band with trumpets and guitars played late into the evening, as I whirled in my billowing white dress with my father. I leaned on my husband's broad shoulder as the band played our favorite love songs. The wine was sweet, our enchiladas, delicious.

A perfect wedding.

I snuggled close to Juan, and he stroked rice from my hair as we roared away in his '59 Chevy. Our three-day honeymoon was a perfect start to our lives as husband and wife.

❧❧❧

"Elena, we need to talk to you."

Just home from our honeymoon the night before, Juan's kiss still lingered on my lips after I sent him out the door to work that morning. I studied Juan's father and mother's dispirited expressions curiously. His mother's eyes were red, like she had been crying. "Our Juan is in trouble. He's in jail."

I dared not breathe for a moment. "What? Was he drinking? What's going on?"

"There was a warrant for his arrest," Juan's father said. "But we don't believe what the police are saying he did!"

## MASTER IN THE MESSAGE

I sat down on the couch, silent, waiting. No one spoke. I finally had to ask it. "What do they say he did?"

"Well, he's *accused* of being part of a ... rape."

*Dios, mio.*

"When was this?" I felt tears welling up behind a dam of confusion in my heart.

"They say about six months ago. BUT WE KNOW IT'S NOT TRUE!"

When my in-laws left, I called my mother, her words ringing in my ears: "He'll never be a good husband ..." But she empathized, crying with me — and for me.

In the next few months of turmoil, I tried to piece together *when* my husband could have been in San Diego, where the alleged crime was committed. Where was I at the time? Planning my wedding? Choosing my wedding gown?

After making bail, he tried to tell his version of the story, but I couldn't shake the feeling he was hiding something.

His parents never lost faith in their Juan and believed him to be innocent all through the months of trial for the gang rape of a young woman. Two men among the three alleged perpetrators invited the jury's disgust. My Juan was called "an accomplice."

News reporters described the crime in detail and dogged the trial daily, writing and reporting on TV with morbid fascination. Shame followed me to the grocery store, and I lay in bed at night after court, weeping like I had contracted an incurable disease. My mistake was

## DEFYING CIRCUMSTANCE

lifelong; I would never be free of living through this humiliation, even if Juan were acquitted.

He wasn't.

I listened to the verdicts as they were read, my fingers locked on my purse to keep from shaking, and praying to the Blessed Virgin for mercy. But the faces of the jurists told me that the mother of God had forsaken Juan and me. The two principle rapists received several years; Juan would be away for a year before receiving probation.

Officers escorted Juan out of the courtroom, and I accepted his sentence as my own. I resolutely smoothed my dress as I stood up with my mother. I was 18 years old and starting to show; my baby would be born while I visited her father in a correctional institution.

❧❧❧

By the time Juan came home from prison, I had run the play a thousand times: My husband *owed* me, big time.

I carried his shame like an ugly Elenaed-wire tattoo on my face, and I was bitter that it wasn't even my ink! My expectations soared high above the steel and razor wire gate as he approached our car where his baby, Julia, and I waited. I had visited him regularly, and the man strutting toward us like a bantam rooster wasn't the man who held me in his arms at my wedding. He grabbed my baby, kissed me passionately and I felt like I had joined his chain gang.

## MASTER IN THE MESSAGE

It had been a very long, lonely year. My empathy for Juan had died along with my memories of childish confessions at Saint Vibiana. No nun or priest could help me now: This was real life — dirty, unfaithful, disloyal.

Juan immediately showed that a good Catholic girl could never fill his insatiable lust. I cried. I raged. I chased his "lovers" off like beetles on dung — but he always charmed them back.

I started using my gift for mathematics at a tax office part-time, and he sometimes stopped by with one of his women to taunt me. But I stayed married because to divorce was "immoral." I knew from Catholic catechism that God would condemn me if I left Juan, and what could I do, anyway? My second child, Daniella, was on the way, a year after he got out of prison.

*Why did Mom have those TV "Jesus preachers" blaring all day long?*

Rex Humbard and Oral Roberts got on my nerves, but their message seemed to inspire my mother, even in her weak condition. Her terminal cancer tore at my emotions while my baby girl kicked my ribs. Why was God doing this to me? I felt stretched thin, like my grandmother's silk stockings, as I prepared Mom's meals and stayed close with Julia, her first grandbaby whom she adored. My father suffered, too, watching his beautiful wife wilt to a shell.

Mother was 37 when she died. Uncle Jimmy, my dad's brother, jumped in to help us with funeral arrangements, and his kindness blessed me whenever he was close. A month after Mom's colon cancer stole her from me, I had my little Daniella.

It wasn't that I hated Juan for flaunting unfaithfulness in my face, but he never owned up to his crime — against me! He showed no remorse for misrepresenting himself to me before we were married. He hid away from friends and family in his cell, while I faced public disgrace. Now he drank and caroused away his chance to make everything right with a wife who still loved him.

*D\*\*\* machismo!*

Even though we battled, Juan and I got close enough to have a third child, while his growing addiction to alcohol turned him uglier toward life.

I learned to gain the upper hand in our arguments and win, but he beat me down emotionally in the end. He just stayed out until morning, and I knew he was sleeping with someone else.

I left for Trinidad and stayed a few weeks to rethink my life. I took Julia and Daniella, while active Marie grew inside me. Grandmother's house, where my aunts and uncles still gathered, seemed smaller. My uncles still tracked coal dust into the house after working at the mines and told their stories of the old days of strikes and wage wars. I felt safe again.

When I got back to San Bernardino, Marie, my third daughter, joined us in our tangled life, and Juan and I decided to separate. In my own apartment, I barely scraped by financially, but Dad helped us when he could.

# MASTER IN THE MESSAGE

Often he came for his favorite meal, enchiladas. He prized his granddaughters like they were gems he had placed in costly settings. Precious. Beautiful. Our hearts were knit closer after Mom's death, and it comforted me every time I heard his gentle knock at our door in the evenings.

"I'm heading for Colorado," he said one day. Trinidad was "thinking ground" for both of us, and I was glad to see him take a vacation.

The girls were all crying at once as he hugged them and me.

"Elena. Don't have any more kids. Okay?"

I laughed and waved him away — too embarrassed to tell him I was pregnant again. My father never made it to Trinidad. He had a heart attack that night.

Uncle Jimmy saved the day again. He chose my father's casket and helped obtain a plot for Dad to be buried beside Mom. I barely held my life together, but I had to, for the sake of my three babies and one more on the way.

*God, you could have taken a drug addict or a drunk. Why did you take my mother and father?*

The good Catholic choir girl, nurtured by nuns and priests, grew angry at the vindictive Virgin Mary she had always revered.

After Juan served me with divorce papers, the courts set alimony payments, but he never paid. I struggled to keep my sanity, working a little, and finally sacrificing my pride and asking for state assistance.

That was the year my beloved Uncle Jimmy died.

## DEFYING CIRCUMSTANCE

Divorced. Excommunicated. Alone.
*If God has forsaken me, I shall live for the devil!*

❧❧❧

But Katrina was my angel. She was a runaway who needed a home, and I needed a helper. Katrina loved my babies and worked cheap. In fact, I had to force her to take any money at all. She became my friend and confidante when I found employment and needed a babysitter during the day. She lived with us, which gave me freedom on some evenings.

"I'll be back late."

At the bathroom mirror, I lined my eyelids, applied shadow and glossed my lips a sensuous red.

"Have fun, Elena. Dance a little for me. Where you goin' tonight?"

"Just out with some girlfriends. Baby bottles are in the fridge."

None of the men I knew seemed any more stable than Juan. I worked with a boss at the tax office who loved to take us girls out to a local eatery and fill us all with Mai Tai cocktails. From the first taste of alcohol, I was hooked, eating *little* on these excursions and drinking *much*.

Some curses, like alcoholism, seem passed on through generations. I had no idea until years later that many of my relatives in Trinidad suffered from alcohol addiction. Even if I had known, I doubt that I would have tried to control my drinking. I yearned for peace in my life, and

# MASTER IN THE MESSAGE

booze deadened my emotions for a short time every few days. It is only by God's grace that I met a good man. Albert and I would be married for 45 years.

☙☙☙

"Elena, don't drink tonight, okay? No one wants to watch you stumbling around."

Albert treated my kids like his own and worked hard to create a home for us. I knew he must really love me to take on my ready-made family. After a time of living together, we married.

But a quiet rage at God roiled into every nook and cranny of my mind, like coal dust from a constant breeze. Guilt and confusion hardened to hatred for my ex-husband, and I stored up old hostility as fuel to burn when Albert and I had disagreements. When he wasn't watching, I deadened my senses with alcohol, the only sedative available for the ache in my soul.

Albert grabbed his jacket, and I put on my most dutiful face as I turned out the living room light. In the darkness, I rolled my eyes over his concerns, and he locked the front door as we left the house.

"Tonight I won't drink. I promise," I said.

And I didn't touch a drop, until my aunt sent my uncle and Albert to buy some condiments for dinner. While my aunt bustled in the kitchen, I found the scotch and guzzled as much as my throat could handle. It burned in my stomach as I waited for a wave to hit my head.

# DEFYING CIRCUMSTANCE

*Ah, there it is. I can get through the night after all ...*

I learned I was pregnant again, and having children with Albert seemed the last straw in my troubled life. I felt so buried in responsibility and failures. When I passed a church, the stained-glass windows reminded me of my banishment from religion. Now I could never seek reconciliation — I had remarried. According to the church, a second marriage sealed my exile from God for as long as I lived. Day by day, unrelenting guilt weakened me, like cancer growing inside.

*No one wants you,* a priestly voice intoned in my mind and only died away if I floated on a cloud of intoxication.

These days, my little sister, Judith, annoyed me even more than when we shared the same bedroom. And her husband, Ray, ticked me off, too. Suddenly *they* knew more than a priest, God's earthly representative empowered to forgive our sins, according to the dictates of the Catholic church. They grinned and preached like crazy Rex Humbard whom I had endured on Mom's TV while she wasted away.

What did Judith have in her life to be so d*** joyful about? Nothing had changed that I could see. I was nursing Christopher when Ray and Judith came to talk to me one Saturday afternoon.

"We're saved, Elena," Judith said. "Ray came back from his tour of duty overseas and told me to read the Bible. It says that I can go straight to Jesus to have my sins wiped away. Then he gave me a clean heart, and I have a

## MASTER IN THE MESSAGE

relationship with him like a *father*. Sister, it's true!"

I glanced at Ray, who sat at my kitchen table transfixed by Judith, like she was the Virgin Mary.

"She tried to prove me wrong," Ray said, laughing a little. "But Jesus got to her. God reached her with his words in the Bible and caught hold of her heart. Mine, too."

I was getting hot, and I stood up. My fifth child was playing on the floor, and my sixth child, Christopher, was nestled in my arms, needing a diaper change. I kept my voice even and decisive. "It's too late for me. The priest says I am condemned. I have no hope. Don't preach this stuff to me."

"But the only true *priest* is JESUS! You go straight to him. He comes into your spirit and forgives you and …"

"NO! Get out! I can't do this right now!" Something bumped against a wall in the kid's room, and I used it as an excuse to leave. "Go. Please, *go.*"

I felt like two cents after they left and wondered, *Who did I send away? Was it God?*

Later, Ray was back at my door. "I am so sorry that I pushed my faith on you, Elena. I'll never do it again, okay?"

"No problem," I said, struggling to keep my composure. I reassured Ray that I didn't hate him and closed the door. The kids were quieting down, and Albert wasn't home from work.

I sat on my bed and marveled at Judith, as strong a Catholic as anyone I knew. Her unapologetic Christian joy glowed from her soul. Ray and Judith wanted me to have this feeling, too … I laid Christopher upon the bed, his face like a little angel, and I tried to talk to God.

"Jesus," I prayed, "if you are real, and everything they say is right, then I want what Judith and Ray have. I *need* to know you, too."

For decades, a dark vesture had insulated me from God's forgiveness. But when I said the words, "Forgive me!" the shroud over my soul lifted. Suddenly, nothing and no one stood between God and me, and it astonished me to feel accepted and free of guilt for the first time in my life.

I looked down at my little Christopher, and I felt different. Raising him didn't seem to be a curse anymore. When Albert got home, I felt different about him, too. I loved him more than ever for his hard work and care of our family.

Albert accepted my religious experience without condemning me and respected the lifestyle adjustments that my new faith in Christ summoned. Parts of our lives together were forever altered, like going out dancing at clubs with friends. In the beginning of my newfound faith, I was clueless about how to explain to anyone the change I felt in my heart.

I sat at Ramon and Olivia's home, a glass of cerveza (beer) in one hand and cigarette in the other, beaming about how Jesus had changed my heart and telling them how to be saved, too. Suddenly, Ramon raised his hand, like a traffic cop.

## MASTER IN THE MESSAGE

"Elena, when you stop drinking and puffing on those cancer sticks, I might start listening to you about Jesus. Until then …" He left the room, and I jammed my cigarette butt into an ashtray, depressed.

At home that night, I prayed, "God, you've got to take away these addictions if you want me to share your love with people. Help me."

For anyone who struggles with alcoholism or drugs, when I say that I was absolutely set free from the cravings — it seems unbelievable. But that's exactly what happened.

In time, I recognized that my whole life was a message for everyone to relate to. I have followed Jesus for 43 years, and I still believe it. At 71, my grueling spiritual contest is visible for everyone to see, and God's Spirit still calls every major play in my life. I have learned to reach deep for compassion, like I strained for the last ounce of endurance in a basketball tournament as a girl. My coach is proving just as faithful toward the *end* of the game as at the *beginning*.

Released from my sense that God was out to punish me for the slightest wrong move, and unchained from addictions, I loaded up my kids and followed Judith to a Nazarene church. I was in my 20s when we attended the Nazarene church for several months. But I felt restless in my soul.

"Pastor, I feel that I should go to a men's halfway house and be part of the ministry there."

Several good people did not understand my unconventional calling, and one long Nazarene pew sat empty the next Sunday. My children and I joined a motley group of rehabilitating drunks and drug addicts at a small chapel outside San Bernardino. God's message of love in me had arrived at Victory Outreach, but again, I was clueless about my coach's strategy.

I gathered up a few other adventurous women to fill up chairs, and I stayed at Victory Outreach until it became apparent that my children needed a Sunday school and youth program to grow strong in this faith that I had found. Judith and I, with our little brood, began attending Colton First Assembly of God, and suddenly I felt like God had placed me in the position to deliver a winning shot.

Ambition burned in my heart to take this message of love into prison chapels around San Bernardino. At Victory Outreach, I had discovered that gangbangers, prostitutes and meth addicts longed for deliverance. God's power worked behind a razor wire fence as powerfully as inside any church.

ے ے ے

"I dedicate this child to you, Lord!"

I prayed this pledge over and over for the nine months I carried Jacob, my seventh and last child. Jacob accompanied me in ministry long before I showed him off in his baby blue outfits at the Colton church. He kicked and rolled inside me, while I lived my message of God's deliverance behind prison walls, or gave my testimony at

## MASTER IN THE MESSAGE

church, or at a kitchen table with an unwed mother.

When Jacob was old enough to mull over his own future, he stated flatly: "Mom, I'm not going to be a preacher! I'm going to be what *I* want to be."

"Okay, Jacob." I chuckled to myself. Everyone bears responsibility for his or her life message. His message and future lay in God's hands, not mine.

☙☙☙

I felt squeezed between the concrete walls at the Riverside county jail, following a uniformed guard. In the narrow hallway, a row of shackled prisoners in orange jumpsuits shuffled toward me. I tried to ignore the chortling as they passed. How easily one of the prisoners might have encircled my throat with cuffed hands to choke out my life or hold me hostage. I shivered a little and kept walking.

It took several months for me to *feel* divinely protected in the company of murderers and drug addicts at places like Glen Halen Rehabilitation Center and California Detention Center. My faith grew stronger over the years as I became pastor to scores of inmates, a shepherd for the unwanted. I could identify with these inmates, because I had been abandoned, too!

With a microphone, amplifier and recorded music (I brought musicians when I could), I preached no frilly, happy stories — but cut to the quick with my message: "I was a complete alcoholic. I lived with guilt that ate at my soul like my mother's cancer. God took away my guilt and shame when I said to Jesus, 'Forgive me!'"

I affirmed my story of deliverance with God's own words from a supernatural, historical book: the Bible. Tears flowed when God's mercy penetrated my prison flock's iron-clad culture of fear and abuse. Their past failures and bitter sentences were no match for the message of Jesus' love.

I look back over my life and remember the struggle raising my children, loving my husband the right way and holding the hands of my "adopted" children locked behind bars. At the end of my "prison time," I often hurriedly gathered up my Bible and music equipment.

"I have to pick up my kids from school! Bring a friend next week, girls …"

৵৵৵

For nearly 40 years, I have loved the throw-away girls and boys in and out of prison. Within my heart, I pray for other Christians to take their message to those shackled with addictions and guilt. The long halls and many steel doors have become too hard for me to travel since my knee replacements. But my unloved girls at institutions like Glen Helen Rehabilitation Center still call to my heart.

Melita scared me.

A string of earsplitting curses spewed from her mouth, rising from the deepest part of her character. Her tirade

## MASTER IN THE MESSAGE

disrupted my meeting for a time, and I left the chapel, feeling like I had accomplished little for God that day.

The next week, Melita stalked up to me and said she wanted to know Jesus! After that, her cursing continued for a while: "You f****** women, shut up! Listen to the lady! She's taking time out of her life to help you!"

Girls poured out of their cells, and the little chapel filled up.

At Glen Helen, Sarah wanted to know about my message. She sent a request from maximum security, through another inmate, that she wanted to talk. After obtaining security clearance, I was escorted to her cell by a burly guard, and I stood at a tiny head-height door with iron mesh between us. On the other side stood a pretty dark-haired girl, accused of a gruesome murder.

"I'm innocent. They're going to give me life in prison!"

We talked for a while, and through my memories of lies and deceit spoken by inmates over the years, I sensed a voice in my heart: *Sarah is telling the truth.*

"You know, I hear girls say that they are innocent every time I come to Glen Helen, Sarah, but I believe you. I'm going to pray for you — and my church, Colton Assembly, will pray, too. God is going to do a miracle in your life, and when he does, I want you to come and testify at our church about your miracle."

I left her cell, knowing that I put God out on a limb. Sarah's eternal life hung in the balance, too.

Months later, on Sunday, a deacon at church told me

that a young woman was looking for me. In a corner of the foyer, Sarah stood shyly, her face beaming.

"Here I am! His miracle happened! I'm free!"

After preaching one evening at a maximum-security prison, a woman I didn't recognize spoke to me. "Elena, you don't have just seven children — I need to correct you."

I smiled, studying her face as she continued. "Remember me? You took in my sister and me years ago! You raised us like your own. I'm your girl!"

And she was.

Over the last half-century, dozens of children have grown up with my love and encouragement, right along with my own kids. Each has made his or her own life-defining choices. Some have accepted God's mercy, while others, to my great anguish, have battled to find their message of faith and hope.

My lovely daughter Daniella fought the demons of drugs and, not long ago, passed away from heart failure while struggling to get clean. When I was a young woman, I called my hardships "storms." Now, my heartaches feel like "tsunamis." It's a mystery how God's power guides my emotions to peace, even through these tsunamis late in my life.

And who would have believed that Jesus would ask me to climb with him to vistas *above* the tsunamis, at my age?

As a wronged bride, rejected and alone, a thread of indignation had tangled itself around my heart.

# MASTER IN THE MESSAGE

Throughout my life, anyone who failed to express proper remorse after hurting me invited my outrage. I thought that they should feel guilty for their offenses. They *owed* me remorse.

In the last three years, I have embraced mercy like an old friend, freeing everyone and myself from any unforgiveness that might encumber relationships. No one *owes* me! No one needs to answer for or regret his or her hurtful actions for me to forgive. God has set me free — AGAIN!

In a class that I teach called Genuine Forgiveness, I never conceal the mess in my message. For 38 of my 71 years, I have lived among my precious Colton church friends, and my trials and triumphs show like a diorama for all to see: my ministry, my marriage, my children.

I know why it's so easy to love others today. The Bible spells it out:

Those who have been *forgiven* much, *love* much.

# CONCLUSION

My heart is full. When I became a pastor, my desire was to change the world. My hope was to see people encouraged and the hurting filled with hope. As I read this book, I saw that passion being fulfilled. However, at Colton First Assembly of God, rather than being content with our past victories, we are spurred to believe that many more can occur.

Every time we see another changed life, it increases our awareness that God really loves people, and he is actively seeking to change lives. Think about it: How did you get this book? We believe you read this book because God brought it to you seeking to reveal his love to you. Whether you're a man or a woman, a logger or a waitress, blue collar or no collar, a parent or a student, we believe God came to save you. He came to save us. He came to save them. He came to save all of us from the hellish pain we've wallowed in and offer real joy and the opportunity to share in real life that will last forever through faith in Jesus Christ.

Do you have honest questions that such radical change is possible? It seems too good to be true, doesn't it? Each of us at Colton First Assembly of God warmly invite you to come and check out our church family. Freely ask questions, examine our statements, see if we're "for real" and, if you choose, journey with us at whatever pace you are comfortable. You will find that we are far from perfect. Our scars and sometimes open wounds are still healing, but we just want you to know God is still completing the process of authentic life change in us. We still make mistakes in our journey, like everyone will. Therefore, we acknowledge our continued need for each other's forgiveness and support. We need the love of God just as much as we did the day before we believed in him.

If you are unable to be with us, yet you intuitively sense you would really like to experience such a life change, here are some basic thoughts to consider. If you choose, at the end of this conclusion, you can pray the suggested prayer. If your prayer genuinely comes from your heart, you will experience the beginning stages of authentic life change, similar to those you have read about.

How does this change occur?

Recognize that what you're doing isn't working. Accept the fact that Jesus desires to forgive you for your bad decisions and selfish motives. Realize that without this forgiveness, you will continue a life separated from God and his amazing love. In the Bible, the book of Romans, chapter 6, verse 23 reads, "The result of sin (seeking our way rather than God's way) is death, but the gift that God freely gives is everlasting life found in Jesus Christ."

Believe in your heart that God passionately loves you and wants to give you a new heart. Ezekiel 11:19 reads, "I will give them singleness of heart and put a new spirit within them. I will take away their stony, stubborn heart and give them a tender, responsive heart" (NLT).

# CONCLUSION

Believe in your heart that "if you confess with your mouth that Jesus is Lord and believe in your heart that God raised him from the dead, you will be saved" (Romans 10:9 NLT).

Believe in your heart that because Jesus paid for your failure and wrong motives, and because you asked him to forgive you, he has filled your new heart with his life in such a way that he transforms you from the inside out. Second Corinthians 5:17 reads, "When someone becomes a Christian, he becomes a brand-new person inside. He is not the same anymore. A new life has begun!"

Why not pray now?

*Lord Jesus, if I've learned one thing in my journey, it's that you are God and I am not. My choices have not resulted in the happiness I hoped they would bring. Not only have I experienced pain, I've also caused it. I know I am separated from you, but I want that to change. I am sorry for the choices I've made that have hurt myself, others and denied you. I believe your death paid for my sins, and you are now alive to change me from the inside out. Would you please do that now? I ask you to come and live in me so that I can sense you are here with me. Thank you for hearing and changing me. Now please help me know when you are talking to me, so I can cooperate with your efforts to change me. Amen.*

## DEFYING CIRCUMSTANCE

Colton's unfolding story of God's love is still being written ... and your name is in it. I hope to see you this Sunday!

Pastor Jonathan Florez
Colton First Assembly of God
Colton, California

We would love for you to join us at
Colton First Assembly of God!

We meet Sunday mornings at 10:30 a.m. at
450 West Citrus Street, Colton, CA 92324.

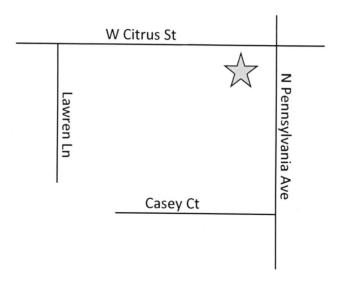

Please call us at 909.825.8901 for directions, or
contact us at www.coltonag.com.

For more information on reaching your city with stories from your church, please contact Good Catch Publishing at www.goodcatchpublishing.com

# Good Catch Publishing

Did one of these stories touch you? Did one of these real people move you to tears? Tell us (and them) about it on our reader blog at www.goodcatchpublishing.blogspot.com.